For the Sake
of the Children

For the Sake of the Children

How to Share Your Children
with Your Ex-Spouse
in Spite of Your Anger
▼

Kris Kline & Stephen Pew, Ph.D.

Prima Publishing
P.O. Box 1260KKP
Rocklin, CA 95677
(916) 786-0426

© 1992 by Kris Kline

Typography by Bookends Typesetting
Copyediting by Linda Purrington
Production by Janelle Rohr, Bookman Productions
Interior design by Renee Deprey
Jacket design by The Dunlavey Studio

Library of Congress Cataloging-in-Publication Data

Kline, Kris.
    For the sake of the children: how to share your children with your ex-spouse—in spite of your anger / by Kris Kline and Stephen Pew.
        p.   cm.
    Includes index.
    ISBN 1-55958-226-X : $10.95
    1. Children of divorced parents—United States.   2. Divorced parents—United States.   3. Child rearing—United States.
    I. Pew. Stephen.   II. Title.
HQ777.5.K58   1991
306.89—dc20   91-7657
                                                                    CIP

92 93 94 95 RRD 10 9 8 7 6 5 4 3 2 1

Printed in the United States of America

For the children—Krista, Stephen, Michele, Tara, Marnie, Ethan, Corey, and Jessica—who remind us of the importance of being responsible parents.

▼
_____

Contents

Chapter 4 Giving Up the Games 67

Are you a player in unproductive games where your children are the pawns? Discover new and more effective ways of communicating, and explore ways to break out of the vicious cycle.

Chapter 5 Situational Peace 93

Even if the bitter conflict between you and your ex is not resolved, you can still create situational peace. Learn acceptable etiquette for divorced parents during public events such as PTA meetings, recitals, graduation ceremonies, and weddings. Discover how achieving situational peace can help you survive these events.

Chapter 6 Facing the Ex-in-Laws 123

Develop the self-confidence to face your former spouse and his or her family and friends, even when you feel older, less attractive, and less well off than the last time you saw these people.

Chapter 7 Including Your Ex's New Spouse 143

Gain insight into the feelings of the stepparents who are involved in your children's lives, and acquire skill at including them appropriately (even if he or she was the "other woman" or "other man" in your spouse's life before your divorce).

Contents

▼
___

Foreword

by Jane Nelsen, Ed.D.

If you are a divorced parent and you love your children, please read this book for the sake of your children. Parents who claim they would do anything for the children they love so much are often totally unaware of how much it hurts their children when they insist on expressing their anger, revenge, or victim status toward an ex-spouse—the other parent. Children need and want to love both their parents, even if they are divorced. It tears children apart to feel they must choose loyalty to only one. Yes, they would prefer that their biological parents stay together, but it's much easier for children to love four parents (two biological parents and two step-parents) than to be forced to choose.

For the sake of your children, get into their worlds. Find out how they feel, what they want, and what is important to them. This does not mean you must give them everything they want, but understanding their feelings and wishes can at least help you be more sensitive and respectful to everyone involved. *For the Sake of the Children* can help you do so, and can also help you deal with your own unresolved issues.

As you read, you will feel understood and validated for your feelings—and even your mistakes—while learning to understand and validate your children's feelings. This book is not designed to make you feel guilty. It will help you become aware of actions that do not serve you and your children, *and* it will help you work through your feelings and deal with them in ways that do serve you and your children.

It's time to deal with the issues affecting children of divorce in a civilized manner. *For the Sake of the Children* is beautifully written to keep you entertained and hold your interest while you gain insights that will enrich your life and the lives of your children.

A Dance for the Bride

"**O**h, and Mommy, I have something to ask you," my 22-year-old daughter rushed on as I began to say good-bye at the end of our long-distance phone call.

Now, as any parent of a postpubescent child knows, when "Mom" or "Dad" is replaced by the endearing "Mommy" or "Daddy," it's time to grab your wallet. This is especially true when, as in our case, the discussion focuses on the child's upcoming marriage.

From the moment of her engagement announcement six months earlier, we'd been caught in an endless swirl of wedding plans. Now, with a mere six months to go, the details had become an integral part of our lives, like brushing our teeth and taking out the garbage. Living hundreds of miles from my daughter hadn't made coordination any easier, and although she and her fiancé were taking full responsibility for everything from wedding invitations to music selections for the reception, she still wanted the security and the sharing of her mother's advice.

Glancing absentmindedly at the open clasp on my empty purse sitting next to the unfinished guest list, I encouraged her to go ahead and tell me what she needed.

"If it's OK with Daddy," she started out bravely, "and I haven't asked him yet, but if it's OK with him," she stammered on, now somewhat nervously, "when they play the music for the parents of the bride and groom to dance" (and now hurrying with panic), "would you dance with him at my wedding?"

I felt suddenly deflated. Groping for words and possibly stunned from battle fatigue into a state of acquiescence—certainly bolstered by my inner confidence that this would never come to pass—I assured her that if her father wanted to dance with me he would have a willing partner.

Not until I heard the unrestrained joy in her voice did the shock of what I'd just agreed to sink in. After saying good-bye, I placed the receiver into its cradle, surprised that I had strength to wield it back into its proper position.

Until that phone call, I'd thought I had my feelings under control about sharing our daughter's wedding day with my former husband. Living over a thousand miles from him, and having not spoken with him for several years, I don't think I'd actually faced that he would really be at the ceremony. I'd just assumed that by ignoring him and maintaining a polite distance, I'd get through with no mental bruises or nasty incidents. I'd been sure that keeping away from both him and my feelings would get me through the celebrations.

My daughter (and her younger sister) had already suffered untold scars from our divorce. It is true that in divorce the children accept the blame and often assume the responsibility for fixing the broken relationship. It's appalling that children end up paying for the mistakes of their parents—*my* child paying for *my* mistakes—I felt the pressure of guilt weighing heavily upon my shoulders.

2

I could remember many times, both in public and private, when her embarrassment over our divorce had been all too evident. I felt I owed it to her to do everything I could to make it up to her by making her wedding the happiest day of her life.

I only hoped her father felt the same.

Our divorce had resulted in one of the most bitter child custody cases ever. It had raged on for more than ten years; charges were filed with the ethics committees of both the lawyers' and the psychologists' associations. It resulted in a precedent-setting decision by the state supreme court. It was an absolutely brilliant example of our district court system at its most incompetent: several attorneys fattened their bank accounts, judges exploited their prejudices and showed their ineptness, expert witnesses wielded solid credentials and flimsy ethics, and the best interests of the children got lost in the drama of the court officials' theater. Feelings bled out while the insanity dragged on. Years went by when anger, pain, and rage were everyday emotions.

Finally, as the battles managed to wear themselves out, the wounds had superficially closed. Still, whenever our two girls spoke of their father and his new family, I listened with self-protective ambivalence. I knew how important he was to them, so his existence had to remain of some consequence to me. Any significant change in his life, such as an illness or loss of a job, which would have bad effects for him, would also have effects on them. But although I had to care about him as he influenced my girls' lives and identities, their good feelings toward him still left me feeling resentful and betrayed.

Fortunately my present love and husband of several years said he was willing to support whatever decision I made about the parents' dance. He reasoned that my daughter knew a "different" person from the one we knew (a concept discussed in Chapter 2). She saw "Dad" as the guy who'd bounced her on his knee and kissed away her childhood tears. My husband also saw her request as her way of trying to mend feelings between her father and me. Because he could see the situation from this perspective, he said he could do anything for a couple of days to make her happy. I wasn't surprised—he had struggled through years at my side in and out of court, giving me both tremendous emotional and financial support, and now his generous attitude gave me courage. (But *he* didn't have to dance with the father of the bride.)

It was certainly ironic that I had in fact gone to a wedding not long before, where the parents of the bride had been divorced for years. When it came time for the parents' dance, the bride's father asked his former wife to be his partner. She turned him down flat. It was awkward and embarrassing for everyone.

I've been through more than one situation with friends who've denied themselves and their children their presence at important occasions altogether. They felt they simply couldn't be in the same room with their ex-husbands or ex-wives.

I decided to write *For the Sake of the Children* because I understand the emotional wounds and buried resentments that surface when seeing an estranged ex-spouse. Old feelings of hate, revenge, and self-protection emerge. Yet there are very good reasons to make these occasions complete and fulfilling for everyone. Your children may have accepted that the marriage won't be mended, yet it may reassure them to see that uncivil behavior need no longer prevail.

Today, blended families have become the rule rather than the exception. Yet divorce behavior has largely remained uncivilized and sometimes cruel. It's not hard to understand why, when we realize that most marriages end through an adversary proceeding—that is, a fight or contest. We're advised to communicate only through our attorneys, and we're encouraged to say whatever it takes to "win." Often our children are coached by attorneys and "experts" to do the same.

Later the rules change again, but this time there are no guidelines. Our children ask—and social occasions demand—that we divorced parents now interact in a positive manner. New methods of communication and social etiquette have to emerge. This is very hard—but essential—if we are to fulfill our roles as parents.

Jessica was an 11-year-old who had studied piano for four years. Her teacher suggested inviting one of her parents to join her in a four-hand duet for the spring recital. Jessica was thrilled. Although neither of her parents played the piano, her stepmother did. Her father suggested that Jessica invite her stepmother to play. "I was nervous about what Mom would say, but it was an honor to play with one of your parents at the recital, and besides, I thought it would be fun. When I asked Sue, my stepmom, if she'd do it, she said she'd love to.

"We were great, and it gave me an excuse to spend more time than usual with my dad, even if he wasn't my partner.

"Mom was terrific about it, which was really a first where my stepmom was concerned. Mom even called and thanked her for doing it. I couldn't believe it. I used to be afraid to even mention *Dad's* name in the house, let alone Sue's."

The fact was that Jessica's mother, Dena, had felt threatened by her only daughter's warm feelings for her ex-husband and his wife. Jessica had responded by hiding her love for them from her mother, thus playing the role of the emotional protector. Fortunately, Dena was able to gain enough self-confidence over the years in her own role in Jessica's life to free her daughter to express herself without guilt. It wasn't easy for Dena. But she was finally able to set aside her pain and take pride in her daughter's musical accomplishments.

* * *

In my own case, I really did hear the intense jubilation with which my own daughter phoned me back to say her father had agreed to be my dance partner at her wedding. Clearly she was still trying to mend the break in our relationship. She had accepted that the marriage itself was over; it was simply important that we acknowledge the past love that had created her. She sounded so tickled that I even managed a lukewarm "How nice" before changing the subject.

I couldn't remember how long it had been since I'd even spoken with the man. Three years? Four? It had been at least five years since I'd seen him, and many more than that since we'd had any civil words. I felt I had every right to feel pure hostility and anger toward him. I'd suffered in anguish for years. The last few years had been easier, but that had been due to distance and avoidance rather than to any real emotional healing. Except for an occasional comment from the girls about their father, he'd ceased to exist for me.

Now, here he was, back in my life.

I dismissed the possibility that my ex-husband would change for those few days, though that certainly would have been my first choice. I could close my eyes and visualize how wonderful it would be to simply wave a magic wand and have him turn into the kind of unselfish, supportive parent and ex-husband I had always wanted him to be— the kind who want the children to adore their mothers, who want to pay for their children's college educations, who wouldn't have bad thoughts about their former spouses. But I knew the clue to making myself feel comfortable with the situation would have to come from within me. I would have to transcend my feelings about him, in hopes that it would help my children and me.

From my personal searching and research, and the insights and experiences I gathered, I discovered how many others needed a book like this. The result is this compilation of personal growth experiences, insights collected from the children of divorced parents and the parents themselves, case histories of the patients of my research and professional colleague Stephen Pew, Ph.D., and his techniques for coping with and lessening the stress of a hostile relationship with the "other parent of your child." You'll learn techniques for working out your own hostilities toward your former spouse, *even if that person remains exactly the same.* You'll acquire skills to help you master your complex feelings about him or her and to make peace with yourself.

In both private practice and public service, Dr. Pew has seen that many personal, career, and even physical problems can be traced back to unresolved conflicts left over from a painful divorce. This book offers techniques to teach you how to get rid of these conflicts. You'll learn how you can talk yourself into just about anything, and how important this concept is to your overall health. You'll acquire the skills through neurosemantics to rethink how you want to behave in your world, and then how to reshape your behavior in a positive manner, resulting in a healthier future!

In recent years scientific evidence has led people to accept that how we think and feel affects our health. One example is the affect of hostility on the immune system that protects us against viruses, bacteria, and other sources of infection. When our bodies are busy reacting to emotional or physical stress, they produce adrenalin, a hormone that provides the body with immediate energy to deal with what we find threatening. But adrenalin may simultaneously reduce our immunity. The good news is that how we react to emotional stress can greatly influence our production of adrenalin. We can learn to manage our emotional stressors (as discussed in Chapter 3) and thus reduce our chance of illness.

Spending such intimate experiences as the wedding of your child with your ex-spouse can be such a stressful event.

It was for John. A man in his 50s and divorced from his children's mother for fifteen years, he found it emotionally impossible to attend his daughter's wedding ceremony. He's still upset about it, and suffers from tremendous guilt and anxiety. He said his daughter expressed hurt and rejection because of his absence, and their relationship has suffered from it. Yet, as much as he regrets missing the wedding, he maintains he simply couldn't do it.

"I know I should have been there, but it was going to be all of Joyce's [his former wife's] family and friends. I'd have been sitting there at a table all by myself. Maybe it was wrong," he admitted, "but I just couldn't face it."

One of the saddest aspects of John's situation is that his decision not to attend was an opportunity forever lost. No set of circumstances can ever give him the chance to go back and attend that wedding. His absence is a hurtful memory for both John and his daughter. Yet the thought of him sitting there alone among his former wife's family and friends was just too terrifying for him to confront. Regardless of how John now comes to terms with himself, he will always be without the loving, sharing experience that he might have enjoyed.

Although this book is designed to help you deal more comfortably with your former spouse where your children are involved, it is *not* designed to be a cure for your animosity. Some of your hostility is no doubt based on a legitimate dislike. In fact, you may well gain an even better understanding as to why you and your ex are no longer together. But by learning to break your old emotional patterns, you'll find yourself unloading a lot of unresolved tensions and resentments. You'll not only gain a greater inner peace, but by showing a little forgiving behavior and compassion, you will help your children grow up with less conflict and a better chance of finding happiness.

Nancy was extremely nervous about how her parents would get along at graduation ceremony. "My father has a real sarcastic sense of humor," she told me, "and I was just waiting for something to explode. When everything went smoothly," she continued, "I was so relieved I broke into tears.

"My stepmother chose not to come, and I appreciated that," Nancy revealed. "I think it made it easier for my mom." Although Nancy expressed affection and devotion for her stepmother, and a sincere concern for her feelings, it was most important to Nancy that both her natural parents were there, and that they seemed happy.

The importance of the parents' relationship was expressed poignantly by Marie, a 19-year-old whose mother and father were divorced when she was 3. "My mother and dad were both remarried within a year of their divorce," she said. "I love my stepfather and my stepmother both very much," she added happily. "I know my parents would have been miserable if they'd stayed together, and would probably have made my life miserable, too," she continued, showing good insight for someone so young.

"But for a long time, even into my teens, I used to have this recurring dream. My mother and stepdad would meet with my father and stepmom," Marie recounted, "and while my mother and father were falling instantly back in love, my stepmom and stepfather fell into love at first sight." The wish was so important to Marie that for her eleventh birthday present she asked her father and

9

stepmother to fly into the town where she lived with her mother and stepfather and join the three of them for dinner. "None of them had a clue as to what I was up to," Marie laughed. "I'm sure I didn't really think it would work. But even though I wasn't terribly disappointed when it didn't," she remembered, "I still occasionally had my dream."

Luckily for Marie, her plan had worked in its own way. It became the first of many joint efforts between both sets of parents to give her the security of a cohesive unit of love and concern for her needs.

Was this harmony and cooperation between her parents easily accomplished? Not according to them. Her mother and father had many old hurts and anxieties to work out, along with the everyday problems facing divorced parents such as financial disagreements, visitation or access conflicts, and differences of opinion on how to raise a child.

Marie's parents may not always consider themselves friends, but they do work at behaving in a friendly manner. They both say they're relieved they could desensitize themselves to annoying personality traits they see in each other.

This process of desensitizing and preparing yourself to share your child's life involves both awareness and personal growth. If I have any regret about this book, it's that I didn't have its information years ago, when my girls were growing up. For me, my children, their stepparents, and my ex-husband, there were scores of missed activities that could have been shared by everyone. For years I carried an unhealthy weight of emotional debris. My children could have been saved so much inner conflict and turmoil. But that's in the past, and looking forward is what is important to me today. Thanks to the information in *For the Sake of the Children,* when the time came I was able to experience the full pleasure of my daughter's wedding day.

And that was with full awareness that I had a dance partner waiting . . .

Which turned out to be a rather pleasant experience. After fifteen years of bitter words and accusations, the children's father reached back into his memory bank to find a few wonderful memories from our marriage. Remarkably, they were times I too have never forgotten. Although I knew that we were both under the full scrutiny of every eye in the place, some waiting impatiently for the music to finish and others curious about what might occur, this dance was for our child, our children, and a tribute to the reality that they were each part him; part me.

Seeing the two of us out on the dance floor, touching and talking, sharing the most important event in her life together, made a complete wedding day for our daughter.

And yet only six months earlier, I'd have said this one dance wasn't even possible.

▼
Chapter

2

Communicating
Without Condemning

Seven-year-old Billy was in love. It was the first time
Cupid's arrow had struck his young heart, and as with all
first loves, it was innocent and pure. Whenever he gazed
on her, he saw a golden-crowned princess. To Billy, her
voice was as smooth as his grandma's vanilla custard. Her
gentleness rivaled that of a fairy godmother. Her name
was Mrs. Daniels, and she was his second-grade teacher.

Ah, the bliss of education. Each morning Billy jumped
out of bed energized by love. He dashed into the bathroom,
where he carefully brushed each and every tooth, just the
way the dental hygienist had taught him. He scrubbed his
face so hard it flushed. He took his pocket-sized comb and
dampened his sandy-colored hair, parting its locks over
and over until he got it divided evenly down the left side
of his small head. Finally, he climbed up onto the toilet
seat, reaching high above his head to the shelf where his
dad kept the shaving lotion Billy had given him for
Christmas. Ever so carefully he lifted it down, cradling it

in his chubby hand with infinite care. He twisted off its cap and poured ever so small a drop into the palm of his left hand. Never taking his eyes from the golden pool as it swam precariously in his hand, he set the bottle down on the bathroom floor. Then he leaned over the sink, clapping his hands together like he'd seen his father do a hundred times, and gingerly patted his freckle-drenched cheeks with the syrupy scent.

How manly he felt!

Carefully replacing the evidence, he hurried back into his bedroom where he donned the clothes he'd so purposefully chosen the night before, and headed downstairs for breakfast.

Billy's parents were well aware that their son had begun to emanate a new odor. They'd even figured out its source, and they'd chosen to ignore it. For along with the new aroma, a whole new attitude had sprung from Billy. Following a less than exemplary first-grade year in school, he was now doing excellent work. His parents, aware that Carolyn Daniels had a reputation as an excellent teacher, realized that Billy also adored her. So Billy's parents overlooked the heavy scent that clung to their son and focused instead on his newly developed interest in school.

Each morning after breakfast, Billy's father walked him to the school bus stop where, depositing Billy safely onto the bus, he was then picked up by Tom, a co-worker in his office, and carpooled to work.

On one such morning in late autumn, Billy's father noticed that Tom was extremely agitated. He asked him if there was anything wrong.

"It's that bleached blonde witch I'm married to," Tom hissed, exploding with pent-up emotion. "I've put up with her lousy cooking, her dogmatic feminism, and her bitchy mother for five years without a complaint. She tells me last night she wants a divorce. That's the thanks I get. Of all the ungrateful rags, she takes the cake. And you know the worst part? The worst part is that she's such a phony. Everybody thinks she's so great. 'Carolyn's such a sweet-heart.' 'Carolyn's so dedicated.' Even from you: 'Carolyn's done so much for Billy.' Take my word for it, Old Buddy, Carolyn Daniels is a raving bitch."

Is it possible that this "dogmatic feminist," this ungrateful wife, this "phony," could be the same Carolyn Daniels that Billy knew as a kind, gentle-tempered educator who had turned him into a real student? If so, whose assessment of Carolyn was right? Was Billy merely a naive child, unable to see through Carolyn's deceitful mask into her true, rotten nature? Or was Tom, hurt by her seeming disregard for their marriage, incapable of seeing who his wife really was?

The fact of the matter is that both assessments were fairly accurate, when taken from the perspectives of the individuals involved. Carolyn was an avid feminist. She had no cooking skills, few housekeeping skills, and no interest in developing either. Tom considered these capabilities important in a wife. Carolyn's mother, a very demonstrative woman, had demeaned Tom during his and Carolyn's entire marriage, and Carolyn had never asked her to stop.

Carolyn was also an excellent teacher. She was inventive, dedicated, inspirational, and fair. She had helped develop new programs for educationally handicapped students in the school district, and she had an open-door policy with her students whenever they needed extra help. She was supportive, gentle, and creative with them.

The point is that Carolyn Daniels is a complex person, just as most of us are. The fact that she lacked many of the attributes that Tom wanted in a marriage partner had almost nothing to do with her abilities as a teacher. Tom cared very little about her teaching skills, and he therefore felt she was greatly lacking in nurturing skills. But

Billy, who had no interest in either Carolyn's homemaking capabilities or her marriage skills, perceived her as *very* nurturing. Furthermore, her relationship with Billy helped him acquire a healthy, positive attitude toward learning.

Should Billy's parents now try to convince their son that from now on he should change his feelings about Mrs. Daniels, *whether or not what Tom Daniels said was true?* Billy's perception of his teacher was appropriate for his age. Even the fact that he idolized this imperfect person was well within normal behavior. It would have been disruptive and possibly destructive to burden Billy with "The Truth" about his teacher. From Billy's standpoint, there was nothing to be gained by his parents enlightening him with their new insight on his teacher, and so they continued to deal with her from Billy's perspective.

It was probably easier for Billy's parents to stick to this concept than it will be for you when dealing with your ex-spouse, particularly if there are still open wounds. But the concept itself of dealing with your child's perception of another person, *especially* when that other person is also a parent, remains just as valid.

Children have an amazing ability to sort things out when they're ready to accept them. You can rest assured that when the time comes, your children will recognize the faults of your ex-spouse without your help. The down side, of course, is that they'll recognize your faults as well, and no amount of hiding will change this fact. It will be far better for the relationship between you and your child if it's not muddied by accusations and innuendos you've made against the other parent.

Children are extremely forgiving of their parents' behavior. They want to see the good in their parents, because it reflects on the good they feel about themselves. In a child's search for self-identity, he (let's say it's a boy) looks to each parent for a beginning. If he is bombarded with enough negatives from one parent about the other, he may begin to believe them, at least for a while. Because of the child's strong identity with each parent, he will now believe that if one of his parents is bad, then he must be at least "half bad," as well. The child, who may well already be wondering what bad thing he did to cause the divorce in the first place, is now faced with the added guilt of being an inherently bad person.

Even if the child doesn't assume the responsibility for the "badness" of the other parent, he will certainly be thrown into a state of conflict if what he's told and what he experiences are discordant.

For instance, a warm, trusted mother tells her son, "Your father doesn't love anyone but himself. If he did, he wouldn't have left us." But then the boy spends some time with his father and has a joyous time. He feels love emanating from his father. He loves his father.

But why, then, he asks himself, is his mother telling him that his father doesn't love him. She's never lied to him before. Is she telling the truth, and if she is, then why does it feel so good to be with his father? Why does it feel like love? Why does his dad spend time with him, roughhousing, playing catch, talking, if he doesn't really love him? But his mother, who clearly loves him, has told him, "Your father only loves himself."

Children need consistency in their lives. They do not need rejection. When you reject something they identify with, you are in essence rejecting them. *Children feel that very acutely.* Adults unfortunately often don't see the connection. To use the example just given, "Of course *I* love you, but your father is a so-and-so," doesn't make sense to a child. At different stages in a child's development, he believes that "If you love me, you love what I love." He wants to know where he stands. When he's told one thing by a trusted parent, but experiences another thing, that creates a conflict. Eventually, he'll be forced to choose, to resolve the conflict. Whether he chooses to believe what one parent is telling him, or what he is observing for himself, it's a no-win situation. When you ask children to choose between their parents, you're courting disaster. (This is explained further in Chapter 4.)

Using children inappropriately as therapeutic agents can embellish these concepts. If a mother and father each try to put children in the judge or jury box to take sides and say, "Mom's right," or "Dad's right," the children are put in the position of the peacemaker. There's often active lobbying to get the children to choose a side. A clue to recognizing this behavior in yourself is to ask, "Am I defensively trying to prove my side to my children?"

In divorce and separation, the children are often left out, or used by one or both parents to get back at the other, or to carry messages, so that each parent can keep track of what the other parent is up to and still can avoid dealing directly with each other. The roles children find themselves thrown into, often by default, are not always healthy. The adults are too often caught up in their own emotional upheaval, and don't take the time to think about or shape the role children play in the divorcing process. The children, too, are caught up in the upheaval, but find themselves quite helpless in how to manage the situation because everything seems to be driven by the conflicting wishes of the adults involved. Children have little to say in what's happening, and this lack of power or influence over the events that are wrecking their lives can add to their sense of failure and despair at their own inability to manage or direct their own lives. These experiences can have long-term effects on the children in issues of power and control.

Avoiding the negative effects of divorce, or of other kinds of loss, on children involved means that the adults, who wield the power, must involve the children in a way meaningful to the children themselves. However,

remember that children won't use the same thinking pro-
cesses as adults. Depending on the age of the children,
they will see the situation from the vantage point of how
it affects *their* lives, activities, routines, and rhythm of the
day. Very young children will be actively attuned to the
emotions of the adults or older siblings, and will look to
them for guidance and security. The older children are,
the more they will be able to talk through or reason
through a situation. Keeping the children accurately informed, frequently informed, and giving them a role in
the divorce situation is extremely important. The role of
the adult is to involve the children at their (the children's)
level of understanding and to provide support, information, and involvement in the process. But *getting the children
involved does not, repeat, does not mean assigning them adult
roles that require them to somehow fix the problem or to judge
who's right or wrong.* If you catch yourself doing this, you
may want to seek counseling. Another alternative is to carefully construct another role for your children, such as "the
kids," rather than that of "a judge," "a jury," "a referee,"
and so on. *The first role of the child is to continue to be a child
at his or her appropriate age level and developmental level.*

Remember, the children, especially young children,
will be watching you closely for cues as to how to perceive
the divorce. The situation needn't be blatant to result in
conflict. For example, Jeannie and Ted split up in late
spring of 1980. Their two children, ages 7 and 9, remained
in the family home with Jeannie, while Ted moved into
an apartment by himself. Jeannie, though very angry at
Ted over the divorce, made an effort not to say negative
things about their father to the children. She also at-
tempted to encourage Ted and the children to spend a
liberal amount of time together.

The problem arose from Jeannie's inability to control her anger when faced with dealing with Ted. She insisted that the children run out to his car when he picked

them up, rather than letting him collect them at the door. Her voice turned to ice whenever he phoned to talk with the children. Because summer break followed so closely on the footsteps of the divorce, the children were home all day and were often privy to Jeannie's phone conversations in which she frequently demeaned Ted to her family and friends. Without meaning to, Jeannie had put her children into the position of hearing "bad" things about their father, while they were simultaneously experiencing good things.

Fortunately for the situation, Jeannie and Ted both recognized a change in the children's attitudes. When the problem came to light, Jeannie sought counseling, where she was able to learn to deal with Ted from her children's perspective of him as a parent, rather than from her perspective of him as an ex-spouse.

Although learning to relate with an ex-spouse from the perspective of your children might seem impossible at this point, keep reading. It may be easier than you think.

First, recognize that at one point in your life you saw some positive qualities in your ex-spouse. If you hadn't, you'd have never been attracted to him or her in the first place. No matter how diminished these qualities may now seem, at one time they were important to you. It's very possible that the same qualities that once drew you to this person may be the very traits that now draw your children so closely to their other parent.

Nancy and Tom were barely out of college when their affair resulted in Nancy's pregnancy. Neither one had planned on a family so soon. Nancy had worked very hard to earn her college degree, and now motherhood was going to end her career before it ever got started. Tom had great expectations of becoming a millionaire before his thirtieth birthday, and now the responsibility of a wife and child threatened to delay his goal.

Yet both Nancy and Tom had been raised Catholic. Neither one was ready to consider abortion. They really did like each other immensely. Nancy loved Tom's caustic wit, his creative mind, and his dedication to himself and his future. Tom liked being around Nancy, with her ready laugh, her cheery outlook, and her artistic taste. For better or worse, they decided to marry, and for ten years it seemed it'd been for the better. After the first child was born, they had a second, and Nancy stayed home to raise them while Tom took the responsibility for the family's income.

As Tom entered his early thirties, however, he became disgruntled. He began to feel that his chance at striking it rich was being squelched by his financial commitment to his family. He began staying out late, drinking and carousing until two or three in the morning. He became short-tempered and nasty, until one day he told Nancy that he simply didn't want the responsibility of a family any more and he was leaving.

He didn't go far. He took an apartment within walking distance from their home, and soon seemed to be the same jovial Tom everyone adored.

Everyone, of course, except Nancy. She was outraged that Tom would dump the entire responsibility of the children in her lap. He'd made enough money for the family to live on comfortably, but now she had to go to work so that Tom could have his own apartment. His relationship with the children was better than ever, now that the responsibility of their meals, their school problems, their ballet lessons and Little League practice, all fell on her shoulders. He was suddenly living the life of the happy bachelor—and loving it. He was always in a great mood when he was with the children and, of course, they adored being with him. Funny, clever Dad.

Nancy's anger was understandable. As a husband, Tom had shown himself to be less than she had expected. Nancy was bitter about having to work as well as to manage all the parental duties. She could feel herself slipping into resentment, and she decided to do something about it.

That was eight years ago. Today, Nancy says she doesn't feel bitter. She's learned to interact with Tom through the children's perspective of him. The children are old enough to realize that their father may have acted self-centeredly where the family was concerned, but they still enjoy his intelligent wit, his pointed one-liners, and his companionship, all without guilt or fear of doing their mother an injustice.

Nancy says, "It was probably easier for me to learn to react to Tom through the kids' perspective of him because he does have a terrific sense of humor going for him. He used to make me laugh until I'd cry, and I miss that. But because I miss it, I didn't want our kids to have to miss out on it.

"My resentment of Tom was getting out of control. I was beginning to feel bitter, and was losing my sense of humor. Every time the kids would try to tell me something their dad did that they thought was funny or clever, I'd feel like reacting with sarcasm. I didn't want to feel like that, and I knew it wasn't helping the kids, either."

The idea of interacting amiably with people without friendship or respect is not new. Most of you at one time or another has had a superior at work, a teacher at school, or perhaps a co-worker, whom you didn't like. You may have thought this person was incompetent, surly, overbearing, chauvinistic, unreliable, or any other number of unflattering things that accounted for your distaste of this individual. Yet chances are you could communicate with this person *well enough to get the job done.* You set your personal assessments aside to interact in a civilized manner. You considered your goal more important than your personal feelings. For the sake of these goals, you communicated with this person from the perspective of your position, rather than from any personal feelings.

Human behavior is dictated by conscious choice. You may choose to reveal your anger at your ex-spouse by screaming, throwing tantrums, name calling, complaining to others, becoming physically violent toward him or her, or by using a myriad of other communication patterns that reflect self-indulgence and lack of control. Or you may choose to control your angry feelings and behave toward your children's other parent with dignity and self-restraint. Your choice of behavior will depend, among other things, on what you want to accomplish.

If you are learning to share your children's lives with an estranged ex-spouse, your goal will center on improving the situation of a fragmented family. Although the behavior of your children's other parent may, in your opinion, break the rules of civility, that is no excuse for you to retaliate in an unrestrained way, particularly in front of your children. To begin with, your ex-spouse will probably become even more vengeful. This downward spiral of vengeance and retaliation only worsens with time, prolonging the bitterness and anger of the divorce long after the wounds should begin to heal. Secondly, if you continue to relive your grievances, they resurface to become just as hurtful and distressful as they were during your marriage. By choosing to bombard your ex-spouse with your anger and frustration, you may be making a stressful situation worse.

Failure to harangue your former spouse with your anger doesn't require, however, that you seethe in silence while eaten up inside by your private torments. In fact, you *must* deal with your negative emotions or the stressful situation will remain and may get worse. (Methods for dealing with these emotions in a positive manner are discussed later.) But dealing with your anger and "blowing your top" are not necessarily one and the same. Learning to re-channel your emotions can benefit you, your children, and the fragmented family as a whole.

Popular philosophy of the 1960s and 1970s held that failing to express your true emotions toward another person, even when those emotions were hostile, was in actuality deceitful and dishonest. We disagree: it is *not* hypocritical to treat an ex-spouse in a well-mannered, civilized fashion, even if you don't like that person. On the contrary, it demonstrates responsible behavior and respect for your children, and gives them a good role model to follow in their social behavior. If you can learn to take your children's perspective, it will be much easier for you to rechannel your emotions when dealing with this other parent.

There is a definite distinction to be made between (1) what can be perceived and (2) what *is* perceived, in a variety of conditions. When you *decide* to perceive a person or a situation in a certain fashion, you use "perceptual selectivity." Your selection at any given time will be based on many factors, including your needs and goals. It thus becomes very important to be clear on what your most important goals are. If your foremost objective in dealing with your former spouse is vengeance, you will select a far different perception of him or her from your selection when your principal motivation is creating the healthiest environment possible for your child in his or her extended family.

Often it is not so much the behavior of the other parent that makes your anger flare, but your perception of what the other parent "ought" to be doing. Does it anger you when your ex-spouse changes plans at the last minute, disrupting your agenda, and disappointing your child? Chances are that you'll be less angry if he or she has (what you consider to be) a valid excuse. If the cancelation is due to an illness or an accident, or is job related,

your reaction will probably be different from your reaction if your ex-spouse is merely choosing to do something
else. However, your child's reaction, particularly if it's a
young child, will be about the same, no matter what the
reason given for canceling the arrangements. Your child
will be disappointed.

Let's say your ex-spouse calls and says he or she has
suddenly come down with the flu. Even if you have to
change your schedule, you will probably do so with some
sympathy and understanding. When you tell your children
that their other parent won't be able to come, you'll do
so with apparent well-meaning and condolence. This attitude transmits to your children a concern for their disappointment and communicates some sympathy with their
feelings.

But if your ex-spouse changes the arrangements with
your children because of a last-minute social engagement,
you may react with heated anger and hostility. Rather than
communicating sympathy and compassion to your children about their feelings, you may be so absorbed with
your own feelings that your children's disappointment gets
slighted or ignored. Rather than transmitting feelings of
concern for your children, you may send them messages
of resentment and animosity that they feel are aimed at
them, because they were the focus of the visit. The children
believe that because they are whom their other parent was
coming to see, they are the ones at fault. They feel guilt
as well as hurt. Just when your children need your reassurance the most, they're set adrift into an atmosphere of in-
dignation and exasperation. This causes further anxiety
for the children the next time parenting time is planned.
Although they *want* to see their other parent, they're afraid
that if he or she doesn't show up again, the custodial
parent will become angry again. Thus the children now
feel it's their responsibility to be rescuers or protectors
for each parent. They must protect the visiting parent from

the custodial parent's anger, and they must protect the custodial parent from the visiting parent's remiss.

In order to learn to communicate with your children's perception of the "other parent," you will want to develop the capacity for participating in their ideas about their other parent. This will require listening to your children so that you can share in their frames of reference. Rather than closing them out whenever they wish to discuss your former spouse, you might ask questions that will help you understand how they view their other parent and what positive qualities they see in this person. Listen to your children carefully enough to understand the feelings underneath the words. *It is important that you appreciate your child's need to feel good about this other parent.* Regardless of whether or not you think your former spouse has a good sense of humor, if you're aware that your children think he or she does, it will make it easier for you to respond appropriately when they relate something "funny" that happened with their other parent.

Think back to a loving adult–child relationship you experienced in your youth. It may have been with a parent, a grandparent, an aunt or uncle, or even a teacher or friend of the family. Choose someone whose attention you sought, and for whose approval you strove. Most importantly, choose someone you loved, and whose love you wished to have and to keep.

Now think about your wonderful memories of time you spent with this person. Let your thoughts drift backward until you can visualize yourself with him or her, perhaps sharing a secret, listening to a favorite story, or simply being together. Allow yourself to feel the insecurities of your youth, and the comforting presence of this favorite grown-up in your life. Luxuriate in the warm glow of reminiscence and remembered love. Think back, perhaps, to an instance when this person stuck up for you against seemingly insurmountable odds, or to when he or she provided comfort when you were hurt or ill. Recall from your past a funny incident or a favorite childhood game. Allow yourself the self-indulgence of childhood adoration. Close your eyes and bask in your recollections.

It feels wonderful, doesn't it? These feelings of loving and of being loved. They are feelings you want to share with all those people who are most important to you. You hope as adults that your own children can look back and conjure up memories of adults in their own lives who make them feel this good. You wouldn't want to sabotage your own child's chances at such memories with people to whom he feels close. You wouldn't deny your own child access to feelings of love, security, comfort, compassion, sympathy, and understanding from someone as important to your child as the other parent. You don't want to undermine your child's relationship with this other parent, because, to your child, each parent offers the potential for security within him- or herself.

When your child's other parent behaves in a manner of which you disapprove, that can arouse an emotional reaction in you. How you choose to handle that reaction depends on your attitude toward dealing with such situations. If you let yourself "step into your child's shoes" before your own emotional reaction takes over, you'll be able to provide your child with a more objective, less irrational viewpoint of the circumstances.

Perceptions of people depend on interpersonal relationships. The qualities you see in a person somewhat depend on whether you like this person or not, as well as whether you feel liked by this person. Most often, you do not like people who you feel dislike you. It is therefore easily understandable why perceptions of former marriage partners about each other are so clearly different from those of their children.

Another tendency when perceiving another person's behavior is to assume that the other person is responsible for the events that are taking place. In other words, if your former spouse cancels a visit with your child at the last minute because of a job-related excuse, you might perceive that he or she is choosing to put a job ahead of your child, while it might be equally valid to perceive that he or she is choosing to put child support payments ahead of his or her own cherished time with your child. It may be equally valid to perceive that he or she has little choice in the decision: this job-related task must be accomplished. Thus, the same behavior may be interpreted as neutral, selfish, or altruistic, depending on how you perceive it.

Because the objective is to communicate with your child about his or her other parent from a less judgmental framework, you'll find it useful to learn to react, not to "my ex," but to "my child's other parent." You are capable of choosing your own behavior, so you have the tools to accomplish this goal. If your first instinct when dealing with your ex-spouse is to "blow your top," interrupt this impulse with a preconceived, practiced thought pattern—*break the circuit* of your uncontrolled response. For instance, to return to the previous example, your former spouse has just phoned at the last minute to cancel his or her parenting time with your children. Your child's face drops, her little bottom lip protrudes, and a tear runs down her freckled nose. She asks you woefully, "Why did Daddy do it again?" or "Doesn't Mommy love me?"

You're instantly aroused with loathing and rage. You're sure if you could get your hands on the rat you'd tear his or her throat out. All the reasons that you despise this person flash before your eyes. Venom starts spewing forth from your mouth, filling the air with anger and hostility. By the time you notice the fear in your child's eyes, it's too late.

Not a very pretty scenario, is it? But what if, as soon as you feel that rage rise in your throat, you have a mental circuit breaker ready to trigger? You'll be able to answer your child in a calm, soothing tone. Your inflections and body language will transmit a comforting, supportive message that will provide some solace. With practice, even your own hostile impulses will lessen.

EXERCISE

Mental Circuit Breaker

To begin creating this mental circuit breaker, practice the following exercises. First, recreate your negative emotions. This can probably be done more easily than you'd like to think. Simply visualize the last encounter you had with your former spouse that "made your blood boil" and disappointed your child. Concentrate on the event until you can feel your anger flare.

Now stop your thought process "in midair." First, focus on your feelings, so that you can learn to recognize them. Once they become familiar to you, you can use them as a warning signal to break the angry behavior impulse. This does not mean that you'll repress the anger, but you'll channel it appropriately, rather than becoming unglued. You'll rechannel the energy into something constructive. Practice this strategy so that it becomes integrated into your behavior bank. The exercise is easy: duplicate the negative emotions you relate to your former spouse, and then "flip the switch" on your mental circuit breaker. This can be done by using a verbal cue such as "*our* child," or "my child's other parent," or by a visualization cue such as an image of your child's face. The important thing is to disengage your anger from your behavior *before* you relate to your child.

This diffusing of angry outbursts may be uncomfortable at first, just as smokers may feel uncomfortable when they give up cigarettes. But just as a former smoker's body adjusts to its fresh, healthier state, so will your emotional response mechanism adjust to a calmer, more serene response system.

Suppose the incident that you're visualizing involves the failure of your former spouse to show up for scheduled parenting time. Again, consider your goal. If it is to create a good environment for your child in which he or she can gain an understanding of each parent and feel free to express how he or she feels, then ranting and raving or crashing dishes against a wall will not accomplish your objective. Neither will a response such as "Yeh, the so-and-so never showed up for me either. That's why I divorced him."

By redirecting your energy, you can use the situation to help your child learn how to deal with life's disappointments. You can let him or her know that it's OK to be angry or to feel let down. You can help your child understand that everyone is a human being, capable of being disappointed or causing disappointment, and that you would be disappointed, too, if your visitor didn't arrive as planned. You can ask your child how it makes him or her feel, and allow him or her to cry or to express disappointment. Perhaps point out that you too are disappointed if your friends make plans with you and then leave without you. You may express your *mutual* letdown. "This is really disappointing, isn't it? Now we have to rearrange our plans. How does it make you feel?" Then talk about it in terms of how *you* feel, rather than blaming your child's other parent for it.

For the second part of this exercise, get a pencil and a piece of paper. Again, concentrate on the last event with your former spouse when you became angry and your child was disappointed. Once you've visualized the situation, write down the circumstances. Write down all the facts that you can remember, and then set the paper aside until your emotions have subsided.

Now retrieve your notes, and try to analyze the event from a different perspective. Ask yourself if your emotional impulses would have been the same if, for instance, it had been in response to someone other than your ex-spouse. Reframe the incident. What if it had been your child's teacher, or an uncle, or grandparent, who had disappointed your child? Suppose it was your doctor or priest. How would you have felt? Would your emotions have been as intense or violent as they were when you visualized your former spouse behaving in this same way? How would have you reacted? Was your response to the behavior itself, or to your perception of what your former spouse intended by his or her actions? Were you reacting to how your ex-spouse behaved, or to how you perceived that he or she "ought" to act? In other words, was your anger based solely on the situation, or was it heightened by the failed relationship between you and your former spouse?

Again, visualize the same situation. This time, though, imagine that you are the child and that your favorite adult (from earlier in the chapter) behaves toward you as your ex-spouse behaved toward your child. Try to imagine how you would feel, not from the position of the former marriage partner, but from the position of the child being disappointed or hurt or even rejected by the behavior of the adored grown-up. Is it fair to say that, as the child, you would want to be comforted and consoled, rather than subjected to a verbal harangue of the favored person, even if that person had disappointed you?

So far we have used examples of situations where your children have been *disappointed* by their other parent. But there are also instances where your children's *delight* with the other parent may cause you to feel angry. For instance, suppose that after three consecutive cancelations, your children's other parent entertains them with a trip to the zoo. They return beaming with excitement. The past three disappointments seem to have been forgotten, and the children are beside themselves with delight over the awesome qualities of their other parent. They're so delighted that they want to give you a replay of the entire afternoon, complete with a running dialogue of everything their other parent did and said.

If you choose, you can take offense at your children's reaction to their trip to the zoo. You can remind them that their other parent didn't show up the last three times, and that after three cancelations, one trip to the zoo is hardly auspicious. You can remind them of all the things that *you* do for them and all the places you've taken them. You can explain to them what *real* parenting means.

Or you can delight in your children's willingness and eagerness to share an important occasion in their lives with you. You can appreciate that they're trying, in the only way they know how, to incorporate you into their picture of the afternoon at the zoo. You can listen to their storytelling from the perspective of listening to a child talk about one of his or her parents. As you begin to react to the relationship of your children and their "other parent," you'll find your emotions begin to accept this relationship as a normal, positive component of your children's lives.

Many parents feel that while "walking a mile in your children's shoes" may work for the vast majority of divorced people, they themselves are exceptions, because they feel the need to "protect" their children from the other parent's "bad" personality. For example, Susan (divorced for three years) says, "I think there is value in devaluing the other parent who is so negative. OK. This is my reasoning: They [the children] don't have life experience the way we do, and you realize there are a lot of assholes out there. *You* learn to discriminate, and not deal with the assholes and not associate with them. They [the children] don't have a choice in the matter. This is their father, or their mother. They *have* to associate with them, OK? But you can devalue the significance or the impact that the bad parent has on their lives."

If this argument seems sound to you, remember that an attack on the children's other parent can feel to the children like an attack on them. If you belittle the children's other parent, it can feel to the children as if you are belittling the children. It is not necessary to devalue the other parent in order to teach your children the values you want them to learn. Children learn by example. If you show them belittling behavior, they will learn to belittle others. If you show them the values you embrace by your words and behavior, they will learn your values. For example, you may feel your former spouse drinks in excess, but you do not need to tell your children that their father or mother is a "drunk." To begin with, what you consider excessive may still be "normal" behavior. Secondly, to tell children that their other parent is a "drunk" may imply to the children that they are responsible or to blame or that you expect the children to "fix" the other parent. After all, children associate themselves with *both* parents, drawing their identities from both their mothers and their fathers. You're discrediting the children, also, when you tell those children there is something "bad" about the other parent.

There is something constructive you can do, however, to guide your children in selecting the values you hope they'll choose. If the issue is excessive drinking, you can teach your children about the advantages of either sobriety or the avoidance of alcohol abuse, whichever viewpoint you hope they will adopt. However, remember that if your behavior doesn't match your teaching, your children are more apt to pattern themselves after what they see than what they are told.

Also, don't manufacture a value system especially designed to devalue your child's other parent. For instance, again using alcohol as an example, Peter and his wife had custody of his two children, ages 6 and 9. He decided to shatter the relationship the children had with their mother and her husband. One of his ploys was to devalue whatever behavior the children talked about having observed while with their mother. One of these behaviors was "drinking beer." Since Peter didn't like beer, yet did enjoy wine, he began setting up a value system for the family that designated beer drinking as very bad, while maintaining that drinking wine was a good moral choice. At the time, the children were young enough to accept this distinction, and for a while actually believed their mother was a "bad" person because she occasionally drank a beer. Fortunately, as the children grew older, they figured out what their father had been up to, and it did nothing to endear him to their hearts. It's not a wise idea to try to fool the kids: it can cause them unnecessary pain, and it simply won't work in the long run.

Resentment and exasperation are emotions that you may well feel toward your former spouse, and you will need to deal with them. However, you don't need to deal with them *in front of your children.* Where your kids are concerned, your *former* spouse is their *present and permanent* parent, and for their sakes, should be referred to with dignity and respect.

One of the most difficult situations to deal with is when your children's other parent refuses to communicate with them. Many parents out there right now may be thinking, "If only I could be so fortunate as to never have to hear from that rat again!" But for those of you who are faced with it, you know how hard it can be. Still, it is important not to bad-mouth the deserting parent, but instead to use your energies to reassure your children that they are not responsible for the other parent's lack of contact. Be open and honest *from their point of view.* If they are angry and hurt or feel deserted, help them to express these feelings of grief and loss so that they can get them out into the open. Once these feelings are in the open, you can help the children understand the situation and deal with it constructively. But be careful that what you're doing is helping them to express *their* feelings, rather than letting them become the recipients of your anger. Explain to them that for some people being a part-time parent is just too painful. Don't condone the behavior, but explain to them that just because you don't see someone on a regular basis doesn't mean you don't love them. In the meantime, keep a consistent flow of reminders about all the people in their lives who do make an effort to be with them and share their love with them. Reassure them that they are loved.

In summary, don't be swayed by the misconception that your negative emotions toward your former spouse are uncontrollable. Practice the exercises for *breaking the circuit* of your angry responses and behavior so that you are able to respond to your children about their other parent in a supportive, constructive manner. Communicate with your children about your former spouse from the *children's perspective* of their "other" parent.

Chapter

3

Breaking Old Habits

Once divorced, you and your former spouse are no longer connected by marriage. You are probably no longer intimate. You no longer have rights or responsibilities to each other as husband and wife. Yet many people try to carry on the routine of the same old familiar, failed relationship as though the marriage were still intact. This chapter shows you how to break old habits and actually form new ways of thinking about, and dealing with, your child's other parent.

Breaking old habits is never easy. It may involve learning to overcome reactive behavior, make decisions, and take responsibility. You may also need to relinquish your quest for control over the other person.

Janice and Steve had been divorced for a little more than three years when their 7-year-old daughter, Mary, came down with the measles. Mary broke out with the rash on the Thursday before her dad's scheduled weekend with her. Because Janice didn't want Mary to leave the house until she got over the disease, she let Steve spend his scheduled Saturday night with his daughter at Janice's home. Steve slept in the guest room.

About two in the morning, both Steve and Janice were awakened by Mary's whimpers. When they entered her room and turned on the light, it was apparent to both of them that she was very flushed. On taking her temperature, they discovered it was almost 102°F.

"She's burning up, Steve," Janice shrieked. "Wrap her in some blankets. I'll have the pediatrician meet us at the hospital."

"Now wait a minute, Janice," Steve said firmly. "It's two o'clock in the morning. Mary's fever is just a normal part of the measles. We're not going to wake up the doctor in the middle of the night. He'll think we're alarmists, and probably crazy as well. I'll keep a check on her, and if the fever gets worse, I'll call him myself. In the meantime, you go back to bed."

They argued back and forth for about twenty minutes, with Janice finally going back to her room to lie awake the rest of the night, frozen with anger at Steve and fear for her daughter. Steve went back to his room and returned to sleep, waking every hour or so to check on Mary. By morning, the child's temperature had dropped two degrees, while Janice's anger had risen.

"I just checked in on Mary," Janice barked at Steve, finding him in the kitchen making some coffee. "It's a damn good thing that child's all right. If anything had happened to her, you'd have been responsible. I'd have never forgiven you."

Janice was furious with Steve. She blamed him both for her bad night, and for his decision, which she felt endangered their child. Although Steve's decision to delay calling the doctor proved to be sound, Janice had really believed Mary was in danger. Yet, in spite of her conviction, she was willing to yield control of the situation to Steve and hold him responsible if anything happened to Mary. In spite of a three-year-old divorce, Janice had reacted to Steve just as she had when they were married. She gave him control of a situation, resented him for taking it, and held him accountable for the outcome. He, similarly, insisted on taking control—the same role he had assumed before the divorce.

A variety of emotional weapons can be used to control another person, such as intimidation, martyrdom, fear, ridicule, and guilt. However, it is imperative for you to understand that your former spouse has no control over you, any more than you do over him or her, unless you consent to it. (The one exception is physical control. If you are physically threatened, call the police. If you fail to do so, you are, in a sense, giving permission to that person to have physical control over you.) We're making a distinction here between "victim blaming" and pointing out that victims have responsibilities. Abuse is not the victim's fault, but it is the victim's responsibility to pull his or her life back together.

In any association where one person has control over another, it is a relationship of mutual consent. Take, for instance, the dictator–victim alliance where the oppressor uses intimidation to get what he or she wants from the victim, and the victim responds by giving in. The intimidator may use disparaging phrases about the victim in order to try to diminish his or her self-esteem. Words like *lazy, stupid, worthless, bad,* and *cheap* are all examples of intimidating language.

Joe is an example of a person with a dictatorial personality. Married for fifteen years, he and Susan divorced three years ago. They have two daughters, ages 15 and 16. Susan described her perception of their relationship during the marriage. "It's very hard, because he's a very strong personality, and he had such an impact on my life. He was in every corner of my life. I mean, I couldn't take the girls out for pizza after gymnastics because he was calling the restaurant or calling the gymnastics school. Or he'd be telling me my friends were talking about me. Really, this is what he did! I mean, really!"

Susan describes their younger daughter, Bev, as having all the attributes Joe values; she's an honor roll student, a born leader, and socially popular. Lynn, however, their older daughter, she describes differently; she's a slower learner, less popular, and more apt to try to fit in with the crowd. Consequently, Susan says, Joe gets frustrated with Lynn, and his way of dealing with the frustration is to belittle her with terms such as *stupid.* "She'll get in the car," says her mother, "and Joe will get critical. Her hair, for instance. She has it shaved a little over here on the side. It'll grow back, but he can't see that. He's too regimental. And dictatorial. And they have a hard time."

Susan, a very nurturing mother, is rightfully upset by Joe's behavior toward their older daughter, but as yet still falls into her old habit of communicating with him as a "victim." In spite of Susan's desire to deal with Joe as an equal, she undermines her own ability. "Joe can be very persuasive, and very charming, when he chooses," she says with exasperation. "No, I let it go," she says, referring to Joe's berating of Lynn, "because with Joe, there's no point in the argument. You will never win. So again, I'm just draining my energies, like I'm a hamster on a wheel, kind of going around in circles."

When Susan says, "There's no point in the argument. You will never win," what she really means is that *she* "will never" win Joe over to her viewpoint. And until she learns to consistently deal with him on a level other than that of "victim," she probably never will.

Kate, however, has figured out how to deal with Joe. Kate's been an acquaintance of his for a number of years, and always found him to be an irresistible business adversary. Then, not long ago, Joe called her for some investment capital. He used all his repertory of intimidation: "Anyone in business today knows that notes are better than cash," "Don't you trust me?" "I can't believe you'd be stupid enough to turn down a deal like this!" "Look at the tax advantages!" This time, however, rather than arguing *his* issues, which Joe was fully prepared to do, Kate came at him from a different direction. "Listen, Joe, I know you're a financial whiz when it comes to big business deals. I wish I had your abilities. But as it is, I'm just not in your league. I don't understand all your high-powered deals, so I'm afraid I'm going to have to say no."

Rather than challenging Joe point by point, and thus discussing the deal in his arena, Kate used a different tack. He'd expected her to argue with him, as she'd always done in the past. Instead, she broke the pattern of their relationship, and literally left him speechless. The technique Kate used to accomplish her goal is based on *neurosemantics,* which is a method of learning how to rethink how you wish to behave in your world. It's also the first step to setting the template for new behavior toward your former spouse in your child's world.

Although it is often enough to say that reality is what we call it, it is also important to note that life is how we think about it. The brain is not merely a mechanical recording device or a playback unit, but the center of all mental activities. It's made up of neurons (hence *neuro-*), about 10 billion of them, that are intertwined in trillions of different connections. Although the number of thoughts we could have is unlimited, certain thoughts and ways of thinking are more likely than others. The neurons in the brain are triggered by experiences and information from the environment as perceived by the senses. The brain receives what the eye sees, the nose smells, the ear hears, the tongue tastes, and the skin feels. As we receive information, the neurons are electrically stimulated and the current travels from one neuron to the next, creating neural pathways. When these pathways are reinforced by recurring information or thoughts, they are strengthened, creating a strong mental image of the information received. (If you want to test this theory, stop now and reread this paragraph several times. You will begin to get a mental picture of the material it contains.) In this way we, as human beings, create knowledge, memories, and a recollection of experience. When we receive new information from our environment, it triggers information stored from past experience. Your own individual combination of neural pathways or experiences shapes your understanding and reactions to the world.

Likewise, our memories of past experiences are stored as the most often repeated images that have come into our brains. This means that as things change, we must experience these changes in order to create new neural pathways to update our information. For instance, if you remember the house you grew up in, you probably remember the house as it was during your childhood. No doubt the house has changed since you were last there, yet unless you have seen the house recently, you have no recollections of these changes because you have not perceived them. If you were to see the house again, you could create new memories or neural pathways to add to your pathways without "erasing" the old ones. We access these memories depending on the information we get from our environment. Much of this information is in the form of symbols.

Symbols help shape the information we access from our brain. For example, if you think of the color yellow, your brain starts to give you a history of your experiences of the color yellow. This free association can lead to other information, such as thoughts about bananas, the sun, or perhaps a favorite prom dress you wore in high school. Words are also symbols. People who study language have made many interesting discoveries about the way words lead us to see and not see certain things, depending on the way we interpret information. For example, people seem to understand things that they have a word for in their vocabulary. If we are to describe something we are thinking about to another person, it is important for us to use words or symbols that are in the common experience of the speaker and listener in order to convey a thought. If the words used by the speaker are not familiar to the listener, then the ability to convey a thought or concept is limited.

In the world of *neurosemantics,* how you describe the world depends on the way you have learned to think about it. If you have a long history of negative encounters with your former spouse, then any symbol that has come to represent that person may trigger those painful memories and lead you to assume that any new experiences you will have with him or her will follow the same pattern. So, if the past several incidents of interactions with your child's other parent have reinforced deceit, anger, fear, and so on, then your first reaction at the thought or message that you will be having a new interaction with this person is to assume that these painful exchanges will be repeated. The brain has a tendency to work in this way as a safety mechanism to protect us. If, in the past, you have touched a hot stove, it is reasonable to expect that, in the future, if you touch a hot stove, you will have the same previous burning experience. The difference, however, is that if you take the time to examine the possibility of changes in the environment since your last experience with it, then you can begin to examine some new possibilities. For example, if the environment has changed (the stove has been unplugged, or the gas has been shut off), then you come to expect something different. In other words, if you look into your own mind (a tremendous resource that is often overlooked), then you can begin to think and discover new ways of describing and behaving.

But if you choose to repeat the old patterns of thinking, which is likely to lead to the old patterns of acting, then you may be doomed to repeat your own history.

Fortunately, as human beings, we are not stuck in the conditioned patterns of behavior we have learned. We have the ability to act differently, even though the circumstances in our environment may appear exactly the same. This holds true for behavior as complex as dealing with your child's other parent, or as simple as an everyday greeting. For example, if in the past when someone said, "How are you," your conditioned response may have been to say, "I'm fine, and how are you?" If you don't stop to think about what you will say or do in this circumstance, you will most likely do what you have always done. But if you make a conscious decision to say to the next person who greets you thus, "I'm terrible, but thank you for asking," you could probably do so. The point is that you have a choice. Although your "gut instinct" may spur you on to act in a patterned or conditioned way, you *can* make a conscious choice to behave differently.

You have a choice: whether or not to recognize the fact that you and your former spouse are no longer connected by marriage. If you choose to accept that premise, *you can choose to break old habits and behave differently toward each other.* The next thing to do is to learn how to make new neural pathways to facilitate your behavioral changes.

As you begin bringing about new patterns of behavior in specific situations, you may ask which comes first, the chicken or the egg? Do you begin by practicing thinking about something differently, or do you begin thinking about something differently because you have gone about experiencing it in a new way?

The answer is "Both." You can begin new neural pathways by either thought or experience. If, for example, you want to create a new neural experience about attending your child's next recital, you can arrange to meet your former spouse for a few practice sessions of spending time together. You can take time to come up with common ground rules and conditions for your treaty. After spend-

44

ing a few hours together successfully, say, watching a movie or listening to music, you begin to have new thoughts and feelings about the experience and add them to your store of memories. These behaviorally reinforced neural pathways then lead you to think and feel differently about the experience.

The reality, however, is that these types of practice sessions are probably not possible because of time, money, or unwillingness. So, given that a series of reinforced behavioral experiences is not a likely option, what alternatives do we have?

If not the chicken, then the egg. You can increase the chances of behaving in a certain way by repeatedly *thinking* about the experience in ways that create new reinforced neural pathways. Most of us, however, spend our time reinforcing the old negative pathways by reliving the painful, perhaps disgusting, past, again and again in our minds. What we are doing is reinforcing the old pathways even more, making them stronger and stronger. How we talk to ourselves, the words and images we use to describe our world to ourselves, have a great deal to do with how we think about the world. If we say to ourselves over and over, "This isn't going to work. I can't do it. I know it's going to be terrible," then these neural pathways are reinforced and we come to believe that it can't be done. Once we believe it's impossible, *it is*. We have created our own reality.

If, in contrast, we mentally practice visualizing positive behavior and feelings, we begin to reinforce old positive neural pathways, or *begin to build new neural pathways* that have a positive bent. By creating these new pathways, and by reinforcing and strengthening them through repetitive thought, we increase our chances of reacting in a positive way when the real life event occurs. We begin to understand old situations in a new way, and thereby have prepared ourselves mentally for the event. This type of mental conditioning sets the stage for new and more productive behavior.

It's easy enough to say that we should do things in a different way. But knowing *what* we should be doing differently and knowing *how* to actually do it are what we must learn. This next section offers a series of exercises that will guide you in *how* you can take more control of your life and thoughts.

EXERCISE

Neurosemantics

The word *neurosemantics* means how signs, symbols, and memories of experiences affect one's emotions and propensity to behave (Stephen Pew).

1. Pick an upcoming situation where the way you think you will feel or act is causing you anxiety.

2. Think through, talk through, or write down your current image of the way you "fear" the situation will play itself out.

3. Carry out the scenario to an absurd amplification, making it much worse than it really might be.

4. Now rewrite the script in a way that you would *like* the situation to play itself out, focusing on the healthy parenting of your children, rather than on what you fear from your ex-spouse.

5. Once you are comfortable with the general nature of the new scene, repeat it to yourself in your mind, over and over. Don't necessarily play the same exact scene repeatedly, but play with a number of variations of the same positive scene. By varying the possibilities, you can become more flexible. Because the scene will, in all probability, not play itself out in the exact way you think of

it, you must be prepared (be flexible) for changes. Don't let changes throw you off, don't revert to the old negative expectations.

Let's play out a situation where you're the non-custodial parent: "Parenting Time."

Describe the setting. You haven't seen your children for a month. Through great effort and much negotiation, you have agreed with your children's other parent that you can take the kids for a weekend. Today is Monday. You are to pick them up at your ex-spouse's house next Saturday morning.

Imagine your prepatterned thoughts (expectations) about how this greeting and picking up the children will work out. Given past experience, you expect the situation to be difficult: tense interactions, the exchange of unpleasantries, name calling, fighting in front of the kids, the kids not being there and you having to wait, lots of passive-aggressive behavior from your ex, reams of directions about what the children may and may not do, an overplayed emotional scene from the other parent at the children's departure, their tearful response, and so on. Imagine yourself in your car on the way to pick up the children. As you approach the old neighborhood, you find you're gripping the steering wheel so tightly that your muscles ache, your palms are sweating, and you're biting your upper lip. As you turn the corner down the old, familiar street, your guts are wrenching. You feel like throwing up or having a bout of diarrhea. Desperately wanting to drive on, you stop in front of the house. As you get out of the car, your knees turn to jelly. You're sure your former spouse is going to be at his or her worst behavior. Defensive anger starts to well up inside of you. As you approach the door, your courage wanes and panic sets in. Your heartbeat increases to the point that you feel you might pass out. As much as you don't want to face the thought, you really are terrified.

Sound familiar? Now make yourself less vulnerable to these emotions, by overexaggerating the situation. Play it out at its unimaginable worst: things really *could* be worse. Start the scene, but all along the way, make it much worse than it really could be. *The point here is to help you realize that the negative image you've created of the true situation might be overstated*—or, if it isn't, that things really could be worse.

Overexaggerate the situation. As you approach the old neighborhood, you find you're grabbing the steering wheel so tightly your knuckles are cobalt blue and the veins on your hands look like a road map. Your palms are sweating so profusely you're soaked to the elbow. You're biting your lip so hard it begins to bleed, dripping blood down the front of your clothes. As you turn the corner onto the old, familiar street, fear grips you to the point that you throw up all over the car seat. Then diarrhea sets in and you soil yourself. As you get out of the car, dozens of people notice how nervous you are and they begin pointing at you and shouting, "Look! It's the *ex!*"

The point here is to strain your current neural pathways to the point where your rational mind declares the image invalid: *"Not real."* Exaggerating your fears to the point of seeing them as "not real" helps dispel the belief they might come true, so let your imagination go to the "not real" point. Conjure up the craziest scenarios you can muster, until you're forced to laugh. The result should be that you come to realize that your negative images have a way of getting carried away to the point of silliness or absurdity. They can build a mental trap for you that sometimes only levity can help you tear down.

Once you've visualized how the visit might actually play itself out, and you've taken your negative thoughts to their own ultimate *absurd negative conclusions*, you have realized that things are not as bad as you might make them up to be.

Rewrite the script. Find a place where you can relax and not be interrupted for fifteen to thirty minutes. Once you get good at building positive images, you can do it any-where and can "speed-scroll" through scenarios in a mat-ter of seconds, but for now, as you are learning to rethink situations, we suggest you start where you can be most suc-cessful. With the lights dimmed and your eyes closed, take in ten breaths, in and out, in a slow rhythm so that you can begin to drain out the stress of the day from your body. It is physically impossible to be both tense and relaxed at the same time. Strong emotional arousal, especially with negative emotions, can interfere with your ability to con-centrate. Remember, your goal here is to build new neural pathways into your memory, and the process of learning and remembering is inhibited when you are under stress. So it is important that you take the time to relax. Breathe in and out, stretching your chest muscles first, and then your entire body. Squeeze your fists tightly together and notice the relaxed feeling you get as you let them go.

Once you are relaxed, start the scenario over again, but this time imagine that you are relaxed, even though you're facing adversity. *Remember, the task is not to imagine that the world is going to change just because you imagined it would, but* YOU *have changed your reactions to these situations, so that you can remain calm and in control and thus able to create peace within yourself and a calmer, healthier environment for those around you.*

You are entering your former neighborhood, only this time you're not squeezing the heck out of the steering wheel. You are calm and relaxed. You are breathing in and out in an easy fashion, and looking forward to the next few moments when you will see your children. As you turn the corner down the old, familiar street, you take in any changes that might have taken place since the last time you were here. You drive up to the house and get out of the car.

You walk up to the door and ring the bell. As you originally expected, you are greeted with a terse, cold comment: "Where have you been? You're late—as usual." The difference is that you are calm, relaxed, and feeling in control and you say something pleasant and neutral such as "I'm looking forward to seeing the kids." You refocus the conversation on a neutral, commonly held issue, such as the real reason you are here, which is to get the kids and have a good time (not to renew old fights and grind old axes). The moment proceeds with subtle accusations toward you such as "Be sure to have the kids back by Sunday morning" (as if you had planned not to). Your past response might have been to retort, "What makes you think I wouldn't have them back by Sunday, Stupid?" Instead, being mentally prepared and having developed and reinforced new neural pathways through your neuro-semantic exercises, you can use these thought patterns and say something like "I'd be happy to have the kids back by Sunday morning. Would 10 A.M. be all right with you? I know they have other schedules to keep."

If this response pattern initially sticks in your throat, remember, the idea here is not to win an argument or a battle of wits with your former spouse. The purpose of your being there is to see your children. That is your focus. Your children love both of you. Bearing that in mind will help you loosen the initial tightness in your throat so that you can practice keeping the situation neutral.

You have the ability to create your own future by the way you think about it. You have a brilliant, creative mind, and you are going to use it constructively so that you can share your children's world with your former spouse. Remember, it is not necessary for the other person to change, for you to learn to change *your* behavior. The reality is that had you actually had the power to change your former spouse, you'd probably still be married! But you *can* learn to behave toward this other person in a healthy, constructive manner, which will help create a more positive environment for your children. As a human being, you are capable of making changes. You have the ability to grow and overcome your mental traps based on old behavior. You do not have to be enslaved by the feelings and experiences of the past, and you do not have to spend $1 billion on long-term therapy to accomplish these changes. *You are in control.* You are in charge of your own life, thoughts, and destiny. You can do this.

Practice the new scenario and strengthen the neural pathways. Once you have built these new ways of responding, you will need to go over them again and again until they feel comfortable. Remember, you don't want to limit yourself to one positive way of doing or saying things. Give yourself several options. You don't have to memorize exactly what you are going to say, but you need to ingrain in your mind that you will say something positive. If you only memorize one thing to say, and it doesn't fit the situation, you will find yourself not knowing your part in the script. Think of several scenarios as a way of telling your mind that you can behave and speak positively, even in the face of adversity. Then practice. Comprehensive practice of a new skill will build confidence in performing that skill, and increasing your confidence will help you to remain calm and relaxed. Remember, neurosemantics is the relationship between symbols and memory, and you are learning to examine and create new symbols in your mind by mentally stating the situation in a new context.

Explore the What if's. What if your former spouse says, "The children are upstairs. I want to discuss your child support payments before I call them down"? This is a topic that should be discussed at an arranged time and place; not off the cuff, and not when the children are present. Chances are it's a very volatile issue, one that can make your defenses tighten the moment the subject comes up. However, this time you're not going to give into that "gut instinct" reaction. Instead, you're going to remain calm and focused on the reason that you're here, which is, of course, to pick up your children. One neutral way to respond to your former spouse might be "Let's set up a time to discuss it. If you'd like to talk about the payments face to face, why don't we meet somewhere for lunch next week. What's your schedule?"

Or what if your former spouse says, "I see you got a new car. I told you last week the kids needed new winter coats, and you said you couldn't even afford to buy them jackets. Now I see why. Your priorities stink." Again, it's a timing issue, and even if the car being referred to is a company car, this is not the time to discuss it. Instead, remaining relaxed and centered on picking up your children, you're going to give a civil, focused reply. One such neutral response might be "I have a full weekend planned for the children, and we really need to get started. If you'd like to discuss these issues, I'd be glad to talk with you next week when we both have more time. What would be a good day?"

Or what if your former spouse says, "I hope you're not going to expose those kids to that bastard [or whore] you're living with." There is no point now in starting to defend the person you're living with. Besides, it probably won't do any good, and will no doubt escalate your former spouse's agitation. Instead, again, stay calm and focused while addressing the issue of your parenting time. An appropriate response might be "I plan on spending the entire weekend with the children. I've been looking forward to spending time with them all month."

The foregoing is just one example of one situation around which these exercises may be designed. This one dealt with anxieties a noncustodial parent may face. However, these same exercises can be constructed around this same situation for a custodial parent, dealing with issues such as the noncustodial parent's late arrival, or accusatory remarks about how the child support payments are being spent, or slanderous remarks about other people in your life. They can also be constructed around any number of other different, difficult situations in which you have to interact with your ex-spouse. It may be pragmatic to choose the very next interactive situation you're scheduled for with your former spouse as a starting point for your exercises.

In creating new symbols and developing new patterns of behavior in a relationship, it is important to learn to develop your verbal communication into neutral, factual, nonblaming statements. One cardinal rule to remember is that it is usually more productive to begin a sentence with words such as "I feel . . ." rather than the word "You . . ." For example, it is much less threatening for a listener to hear the phrase "I feel the children would enjoy seeing more of you" rather than "You should see the kids more often."

Remember, the objective here is to communicate in a nonblaming way and avoid setting up a situation where the other person feels the need to defend his or her actions. In Chapter 2 we discussed the analogy of professional or business behavior to personal situations. Follow the etiquette of the work environment when interacting with your former spouse. Tact, poise, and carefully thought-through phrasing are commonplace rules in work or professional situations. Recognizing the other person as a partner, associate, or co-worker denotes a different mind-set from that we often adopt in our personal lives. Yet this is exactly what a healthy divorce creates: a partnership where the goal or job is that of raising the children. When it comes to our personal and intimate interactions, the phrase "familiarity breeds contempt" can be reconceptualized as "familiarity breeds a lack of good manners." Through the divorcing process, new mind-sets must be exercised in order to create the basis for new rules and manners for interaction.

Thus instead of making blaming or inflammatory statements such as "you didn't tell me . . . ," less threatening phrasing can be substituted, such as "I'm sorry, it was not my understanding that . . ." Here are some blaming and nonblaming models to help you develop a new mindset or manners for communication.

- "How can we make this work better for both of us?" rather than "You should have been more careful."

- "What can I do to help this situation?" rather than "If only you would . . ."

- "It doesn't appear that our schedule is working out as agreed. How can we come up with a schedule that works for both of us?" rather than "You're always late getting the kids back. You do this just to hurt me."

Notice that this switch requires some rethinking on your part. Your first task is to take your feelings out of the context of blaming the other person for the way you feel. Next, adopt the mind-set of coming up with solutions to the problem that are mutually satisfying. Now that we have given you some examples, it is your turn to apply this knowledge to your own situation.

EXERCISE

Develop Nonblaming Statements

Find thirty minutes in your schedule where you will not be interrupted. Write down all the "blaming . . . you" statements that you are exchanging with your former spouse. Now, write down some possible nonblaming phrases and practice them. Imagine situations where the nonblaming statements can be used, and imagine yourself using them with a great deal of comfort and finesse. Practice, practice, practice.

At first, the neurosemantic exercises discussed in this chapter may seem uncomfortable, and the thought of the interaction itself may seem downright foreboding. *But you can do it.* No one likes to be unjustly accused of negative behavior, or to hear seemingly slanderous remarks about people who are very important to them. But these issues need to be addressed at the proper time and place. Remember, you are the master of your own thoughts. You can control your feelings, or not. It will take work and practice, but as you repeat the exercises, and then the actual child-focused behavior, using affirmative words to help shape your environment, the memory of these experiences will be continually updated. Your new, behaviorally reinforced neural pathways will lead you to think and feel more assured and confident about sharing your child's world with your former spouse.

Although it's often hard to empathize with someone we view as a persecutor or a source of pain, the reality is that in these custody-related situations, such as the exchange of children from one parent to the other, both adults, and probably the kids, are equally anxious. Remember, your former spouse is likely to be as nervous as you were before you went through these exercises. He or she may not have had the advantage of having learned new ways to think and behave. In any case, having read this chapter, you are more prepared to meet the challenge than your former spouse is, so in one small sense you have more responsibility to keep the situation on an even keel, because you are now more capable and competent to do so. Remember, also, that your former spouse has probably reinforced all his or her own negative expectations, and has conditioned him- or herself to react defensively and negatively. When you *don't* act as expected, he or she will no doubt be thrown off by your pleasant attitude of cooperation. Although the initial response might be "How dare you be nice? What are you up to?" with consistency on your part your former spouse will learn to trust your positive behavior and may begin to react with a more positive attitude. But more importantly, your children will begin to see constructive interactions between their parents, and will feel more secure in their own worlds.

The importance of this cannot be overstated. Failure to break the old habits of the failed relationship with your former spouse can lead to devastating consequences for your children. For example, David and Cindy were officially divorced in 1983. "It took four or five years before that with the actual decision to split," Cindy says, "the physical moving out of the house, which he did, and the agonies of 'Let's try to work things out,' to moving back into the house . . . try it again. When that didn't work, out of the house he goes again. [It was] just a matter of trying to work through that situation, you know, to split or not. I've been told a psychological divorce had already occurred, and it was just a matter of making it legal."

At the time of David and Cindy's decision to consider divorce, their daughter, Tina, was 4 years old. She was a happy, well-behaved child with a sweet, inquisitive nature. As far as her initial reaction to her parents' divorce, her mother says Tina never really dealt with it. "She just stuffed it. And what she can remember about those years is the arguing. Now she'll say, 'I just remember the arguing, and how I didn't like that.' Not that we would argue in front of her [but] she could hear us."

Referring to David, Cindy says, "I suppose he's a person to point fingers and blame. That sort of thing, if you're a person who's going to accept it." And Cindy says she did accept it. She says that when David was angry with her, she thought, "It must be something I did that made him so angry." She says their behavior toward each other didn't change during the four years of trial separations, nor for seven more years after the divorce. By consistently repeating the pattern of their old interactions, they kept behaviorally and mentally reinforcing negative neural pathways without taking into account the changes in their environment (that is, the divorce). It wasn't until a family crisis arose involving Tina that they finally realized the necessity of re-evaluating their relationship.

"Our divorce was all about possession," she says. "Just possession of person. Ownership. And the feelings that you have when, you know, feelings of 'you were mine and I was yours and nobody else could have you,' or that sort of thing. It was just sick. I think we were dishonest with Tina. And with each other, basically. You know, being able to say, 'We're going to take this step. We're going to get a divorce.' We never dealt with the real issue, and we *were* divorced. We were both clinging to something that didn't exist any longer. That's wrong. We should have been going our separate ways."

Consequently, because David and Cindy's behavior toward each other never changed, Tina never dealt with the grief and loss of the divorce. Cindy explains, "It really mixed her up so much that she never dealt with the loss. Never had any grief over it, because in her mind it never really happened. Other than that Dad didn't live here anymore, and Dad wasn't available to her anymore, all the feelings she had about that went way down."

All through elementary school and junior high, Tina was a good student and popular with her friends. She loved riding horses, and eventually began to show them competitively. Then, tragically, when Tina entered her first year in high school, the years of repressing her parents' divorce caught up with her. She met some other young people who introduced her to alcohol and drugs as a way of coping with her feelings of loss and grief and hurt, and within an incredibly short four-month period, her behavior, before always so charming and delightful, turned self-destructive and retributive. She started dating a young man who soon began terrorizing Tina's mother, burglarizing their house three times in a four-month period. She developed an absolute "I don't care" attitude, both at school and at home. Her mother described Tina's behavior this way. "From September through mid-January, she just went right downhill. She got into inhalants . . . She almost killed herself." Cindy's eyes well with tears as she speaks. "Last year was the year from hell. You know, to watch the single most important thing in your life almost kill herself . . . she almost did. Her dependency . . . it's how she copes with her feelings. That's how she started to cope with her feelings that she'd shoved way down, back to the feelings of loss from the divorce. And she just didn't have the coping mechanisms to deal with those very strong feelings. Add adolescent feelings to that, and you've got a keg of dynamite. As a matter of fact, in chemical dependency treatment, it's a big part of treatment . . . dealing with loss, you know, and grief, because most kids turn to drugs and alcohol to cope with feelings. OK. What feelings do they have? It's generally loss and grief. Oh," she says with poignant irony, "how wise I am at this moment."

Right now, Tina's condition is touch and go. After the episode with inhalants, Cindy entered Tina in outpatient counseling, but at that point the teenager needed more intensive help. "She was having none of it, basically. It got to the point where they said, 'Hey, all the red flags are here. You've got to do something.' So I had all the treatment centers scouted out, and all that. You know, I gave her one more chance, and, of course, she couldn't do it. She was too far into it by that point, and so I had to physically take her in." Tina spent thirty days in the center, and then the next five and a half months at a halfway house.

Meanwhile, Cindy began to get counseling. She has finally broken the old habits of the failed relationship with her former husband by creating new neural pathways of behavior. She's no longer trapped behind the psychological bars that she had constructed for herself, and has come to recognize that her behavior had been based on a false assumption: "My ex is mad at me. It must be something I did that made him so angry. I'm such a bad person." She now sees that what she and David did, by continuing to behave toward each other and interact as they had during their marriage, perpetuated an unhealthy relationship that resulted in devastating consequences for their daughter.

That whole episode began a year ago. Tina, a talented, strikingly beautiful young woman, is now walking a tight-rope of rehabilitation. At this point, it's up to her as to whether she'll make it or not.

Fortunately, divorce does not have to have such destructive consequences for a child. The sooner parents can begin to create new, positive neural pathways and patterns of behavior toward each other, the more likely a new, healthier environment will develop for the children. The example of Nancy and Tom (from Chapter 2) illustrates this point. When Nancy and Tom were divorced eight years ago, their daughter, Melissa, was 7 years old and their son, Jack, was 10. It was not a particularly amiable divorce, because Tom was the sole initiator of the split-up. Before their separation, Tom often stayed out all night, socializing in bars and drinking with friends. Nancy was very hurt and angry. She often stayed up all night worrying about whether he was out carousing, or had been in a terrible accident somewhere and needed help. She always cared deeply about him, and to this day isn't sure that, had Tom been willing to stick in there, they couldn't have made the marriage work.

In the aftermath of divorce, it's often more difficult for the injured party, like Nancy, to cooperate with a child's other parent, than it is for the initiator of the divorce to do so. After all, the instigator of the separation gets what he or she wanted—that is, an end to the marriage—and can sometimes more easily afford to be generous with his or her behavior. (Of course, sometimes the initiator *is* the injured party, in which case it's still the rejected person who usually has the more difficult time adjusting to the divorce.) In any case, Nancy felt rejected and resentful. However, she made up her mind, even before Tom moved out, that she was not going to let her anger at him disrupt her children's feelings for their father. She began immediately to create new neural pathways for herself, refocusing on Tom as the father of her children, rather than as her "rejecting husband." That didn't mean that Nancy's pain and grief just went away, or that she and Tom didn't have their moments of animosity, but it did mean she was able to form a different relationship with Tom, one that focused on the children rather than on him.

Tom was also purposeful in breaking the old behavior patterns. He was, and still is, always careful to avoid discussing any topics with Nancy that might relate to former intimacies in their lives. Although he has maintained a friendly relationship with Nancy, he is simultaneously on guard about falsely misleading her with sexual overtones or innuendos. If he senses a discussion is becoming too intimate, he brings it to a close immediately, changing the subject to something less personal. To do this, Tom had to practice thinking of their relationship in new ways.

Nancy and Tom's willingness to focus on the parenting of their children, rather than on each other, seems to have created a healthy environment for their children. Their daughter, Melissa, is now a sophomore in high school. She's a healthy, well-adjusted young woman who talks very openly about her parents' divorce. In reference to remembering if her parents argued, she says, "Actually, no. They were really good about that. You know, I know people that say they had a really tough time. Their parents did fight a lot, but, no, when I was little I never saw them fight."

Melissa acknowledges that it's painful to have your parents divorced, but, she says, "Mostly, you just have to let yourself go through it. I mean, it hurts and all, but you have to go through it. You can't just ignore it, or it'll just stay inside."

Melissa says that she likes having both her parents involved in her life and in her activities. "It's just nice, even though they're not involved together anymore, but they're still, both of them, important to me, so it's just nice to have them there."

Nancy and Tom have both made a concerted effort to make their divorce a separate issue from the parenting of their children. Melissa says how glad she is that she's not a "message carrier" between her mother and father. "I think pretty much they're able to talk to each other and say what they mean and everything." She says that she thinks the best advice she could give to divorcing parents is "Even though you're going to be apart, make an effort to get along. Not putting on a show, but just for the child, so the child could have both parents around. Just make an effort to get along."

"Just make an effort to get along."

To many people, the concept of love is one of obligation, responsibility, and thus, as we discussed early in this chapter, an opportunity to exercise control over another. This is often evidenced by the use of the phrase "If you really loved me, you'd . . . ," as if the proof of "love" were compliance with another's wishes.

Divorced or divorcing couples sometimes fail to remember that along with divorce comes freedom to do as you want rather than as someone else wants you to (perhaps out of guilt). To truly break the emotional ties of guilt, or love, is to realize that you cannot use your love as a lever to force the other to behave as you wish him or her to. A healthy relationship, whether in or out of love or marriage, does not use the relationship as a lever for obligation or coercion. If the phrase "If you really loved me, you'd . . ." ever came up in a healthy relationship (which it wouldn't, except as a joke), the proper response would be "What leads you to believe I don't love you?" rather than getting sucked into the trap of responding defensively or reactively in order to "prove your love."

The same trap follows if one former spouse says to the other, "If you really loved the children, you'd . . . be on time . . . pay your child support payments . . . let me have my way" . . . and so on. It's the same trap. There are two separate issues here: (1) "Do you love the children?" and (2), "Will you do what I want you to do?" In this context, the issues *are not related*; using them in the same sentence is an attempt to manipulate through guilt and, in general, to start the fights and power plays all over again.

It is important that parents have an open, and hopefully agreed-on, understanding of what kind of behavior constitutes love for the children. Setting the standards for how love will be measured is crucial to the communication between parents regarding their children. When setting these standards, it is important to clearly define the *cues* that each will use to indicate the presence of love. When we go out to buy a car, for example, we look for certain things that tell us this is a quality machine. However, we each look for our own set of cues. You may kick the tires, while someone else may look under the hood or listen for unusual sounds.

The same holds true for love. We all have an internal set of cues that we have adopted to use as *our* acid test of whether someone loves us or not. If the person demonstrates these cues (behavior), then we are convinced we are loved.

EXERCISE

Evidence of Love

List all the things you personally have adopted as evidence of love. List all the things other people do that you have adopted as evidence of *not* being loved (for example, when someone is late or forgets your birthday).

Now make the same type of list for the kind of behavior that constitutes your love for your children: "If I really love my children, then I will behave in the following ways." For example, "Love may mean I love my children when I

1. "Hug them

2. "Listen to what they have to say

3. "Treat them with the respect due to their age and understanding

4. "Involve them in deciding what happens in their lives (those things I control)

5. "Am honest with them

6. "Am truthful with them

7. "Take time to find out and remember what is important to them, and then act accordingly to let them know I know

8. "Don't put them down

9. "Don't use them to get back at my former spouse

10. "Don't call them names

11. "Don't manipulate them to do what I want them to do

12. "Respect their lives as separate and distinct from mine, giving them the opportunity to make age-appropriate decisions for themselves"

Then make a list of what love does *not* mean. For example, "It *doesn't* mean I don't love my kids just because"

1. "I'm late picking them up.
2. "I didn't make my child support payment.
3. "I forgot to call and tell you we'd be late.
4. "I canceled a visit."

"These may be acts of irresponsibility. They may be inconsiderate toward you. They may even be rude or thoughtless, but they are not, *are not,* some sort of self-declared evidence that I do not love my kids."

Remember, these lists will constantly need review and updating as you gain insight into your own definitions of love. Sharing your lists with your former spouse can be very productive if both of you are open and committed to improving communication through this method. In addition, these lists serve their most important purpose as working documents for you to gain insight about what constitutes a behavioral act of love for you. By gaining this insight, you are better prepared to develop new ways of understanding love. A willingness to *stop* using love as a lever to force your former spouse to behave as you wish will take self-discipline and work, *but you can do it.* You can create new neural pathways through the neurosemantic exercises given earlier in this chapter. And you can strengthen those pathways through practice and repeated behavior toward your child's other parent until your new, healthier pattern of behavior becomes your "gut instinct."

In summary, neurosemantics is how signs, symbols, and memories of experiences affect our emotions and propensity to behave. The brain stores information through neural pathways that are strengthened by repetition. The more a pathway is strengthened by repeated or similar thought, the more strength a particular notion gains. These neural pathways become the driving force for our actions and emotions. If you have a memory of a particular person or set of circumstances that has been reinforced often in the past, then your expectation when seeing that person or repeating those circumstances is guided by the past experience. If you want to act, behave, or feel differently from how you have in the past, it is important that you condition yourself and your thoughts in new ways that are more consistent with how you would like to feel and behave, thus taking more active control of your thoughts and behavior.

Chapter 4

Giving Up
the Games

One of the most frequent injustices committed by divorced or divorcing people is psychological game playing.
Although the games and the rules are many, in most cases
the object is the same: the player wants to "win the prize,"
which is getting the child to side with one parent against
the other. These games can be very subtle, and perhaps
sometimes even unintentional, but they can lead to long-
term damage.

Before you dismiss this kind of gamesmanship as
beneath your dignity, stop and reflect a moment. Who
among us divorced parents has never felt just a little twinge
of vengeful triumph on hearing one of our children
choose to be with us rather than with the other parent,
whether to live with us or simply to spend an afternoon in
our company? It's natural to want to be chosen, and to be
selected over an "adversary" can be more enticing yet. A
problem develops, however, when the idea of being chosen

becomes so seductive that the parent manipulates the child and the situation to produce the desired outcome.

One form of this behavior that is popular among divorced parents is the "sideline instigator" game. In this game, which is played by three or more people, one person strengthens his or her own position by keeping the other two fighting with one another. Played among peers, phrases like "you're not going to take that from him, are you?" or "I'd give him a piece of my mind if I were you" are good strategies. The person fostering the fight "wins," of course, when he or she hears about the other person's troubles with the third. Because the other two are always at odds with each other, the focus is kept off the person who is perpetuating the trouble. And the two fighters feel incessant anxiety as they beat each other up.

When this game is started by a parent, the strategy is to keep the children fighting with the other parent so that he or she can pose as the loving and caring protector. Parents can be very clever in provoking these fights or conflicts. For example, one parent—let's say the mother—is less financially well off than the father. The mother takes every opportunity to talk to the children about the evils of money and success. She takes on the attitude of apparent unselfishness, preaching altruism and self-denial whenever the children talk about experiences or gifts they've enjoyed that their father provided. She uses quotes from the Bible to point out the sins of materialism. Note that without ever directly referring to him, the mother is able to berate the father's behavior (being successful) indirectly and negatively. This sets up the children to somehow confront their father about his (alleged negative) behavior. Dad then tries to defend himself, making the situation worse. If Mom can set up an argument between Dad and the children about his behavior, the "sideline instigator" game is off and running.

An example of this game was demonstrated by Ed, a 30-year-old account executive. He and his second wife, a homemaker, had custody of his two sons from his former marriage. The boys' mother, Trudy, and her new husband, Ben, had a successful toy store. Earned by hard work and some luck, the store income allowed Trudy and Ben to buy a large home, with a swimming pool and tennis court.

Although Ed had a good income, he felt intimidated by the success of his former wife and her husband, and it bothered him a lot when the boys came back from time with their mother and talked about the big new house or the good time they'd had swimming, not to mention the new toys from the store. To diminish their mother's success, and subsequently their mother, in the children's eyes, Ed began a holy war against "materialistic people." He set up a value system for the children to teach them the moral virtues of poverty. Whenever the boys received Christmas presents or birthday gifts from their mother and stepfather, Ed made them donate the gifts to charity. As Ed's salary increased, he spent it in ways that weren't apparent to the boys, such as on a membership for himself to a private golf course and on expensive clothes for himself and his wife. In the meantime, the boys were kept under the illusion that their father and stepmother had very little money and that the financial success of their mother and stepfather was somehow immoral. As 9-year-old Toby explained his feelings for his mother at the time, "I don't feel very close to her. I mean, well, she has all that money. And it's like she lives on money. She doesn't live on love at all. She just lives on all that money." The boys began making snide remarks to their mother and stepfather about "rich" people and their lifestyle. This, of course, caused tension.

It also caused conflict *within* the boys themselves. They actually enjoyed the swimming pool, the tennis court, and the big house—which made them feel guilty because they thought it was "wrong" to enjoy such things. They felt a certain superiority and control in condemning their mother and stepfather's lifestyle, but at the same time they didn't like the responsibility of feeling that they had to condemn it. They also resented being forced to give away birthday and Christmas gifts.

Eventually, the boys grew old enough to figure out (with the help of counseling) that their father, Ed, had been instigating friction between their mother and themselves, and was actually financially well off and could have provided for them much better than he had chosen to do.

As teenagers, the boys voiced their wishes to live with their mother and stepfather, and subsequently custody was transferred to Trudy and Ben. As young adults, the boys have developed a solid, open relationship with their mother and stepfather, and have also made efforts to keep communication open between themselves and their father and stepmother. They consider both sets of parents important in their lives.

If you find yourself a fighter in the game of "sideline instigator," you need to get out of the battle. You can do so by addressing the unproductiveness of arguing with your children, rather than by defending yourself against their accusations. For instance, if the issue is the morality of financial success, you do not need to convince your children that financial success is preferable to lack of success. Instead, point out to them that it's OK for you and them to have different ideas about money. Assure them that you'll still love them, even when you share different opinions about things. Explain to them that financial success does not fall into the category of right and wrong, but is more a matter of fact, and facts are neither good nor bad. This is an excellent opportunity to teach them the value of tolerance and respect for other people's points of view and (in this case) the value of money and how it is used.

70

If, however, you are the parent starting the fights, you are the source of the problem, and you are not doing yourself or anyone else any good by this behavior. If you find yourself trying to manipulate others in this way, you're a good candidate for counseling. For the sake of your children, and yourself, get some help as quickly as you can to learn new and appropriate ways of managing your life.

Children are also very clever in the "Let's have Mom and Dad fight" version of this game. By keeping their parents at odds, they strengthen their own position as powerful manipulators. Children are quick studies, and when they observe this type of manipulation done by a parent, they quickly learn to copy it. Here the long-term damage results, although it may seem just that the parents' games, learned by the children, now come back to haunt the parents themselves.

Another variation of the "sideline instigator" game is the "parent to the rescue" game. It can arise when one parent and the child disagree. Although it may be very tempting to become the "rescuing parent," the parent who provides understanding and love and protection, that role can be played in a harmful or unproductive way. Initially, a child may like a rescuing parent to side with him or her against the other parent, especially if the child feels treated unfairly. Think how wonderful it might have seemed for you as a child to have one parent always sticking up for you against the other parent, so you could get your own way. This, in fact, may have actually been your experience with your family, and this could be a game you learned long ago. Remember, most of our training about how to be parents came from those adults in parental roles when we grew up. However, this type of "parent to the rescue" behavior soon raises problems of disloyalty in the child. It also teaches the child manipulation and deceitfulness.

Don't intervene in the relationship between your child and your ex-spouse. (Of course, if the problem is actual neglect or abuse, it's time to seek professional help. Contact the appropriate authorities. But if the child is not endangered, stay out of it.) Encourage your child to deal with the other parent in a results-oriented fashion. Help your child to isolate the issues that are important to him or her, and to clarify the child's wants, needs, and values. Once the child has a clear view of the problem with the other parent, then they can work to find a solution that is acceptable to them both. Working out the problem may be impossible, but that is up to them. Let the two of them create their own relationship.

You can, however, help your child define his or her own relationship with the other parent. When your child complains about something your former spouse has said or done, you can explain that you have no control over the other parent's behavior (just as you have no control over the Sunday school teacher's behavior or the principal's behavior or your own parents' behavior). You can let your child know that you care about his or her anxiety and that you understand. You can show that you understand by talking about your own anxieties about other (unrelated) matters. Then you can assure your child that you are confident that he or she and the other parent can work things out between the two of them, and that they don't need you to intercede.

It's natural for children to complain to one parent about the other one, especially when they think they can thus get their own way. Usually when parents are divorced, each one has his or her own rules about what the children can and cannot do. If one parent allows the children to stay up until ten o'clock, and the other insists that they be in bed by nine, you can bet the more lenient parent will hear about what an ogre the stricter parent becomes at bedtime. However, when a child tries to lure you into criticizing the other parent, *don't do it*, inviting though it may seem.

Here is a typical attempt to draw you into the "parent to the rescue" game. Your daughter comes home from a day with her father. The first thing out of her mouth is "Do you know what Dad did? He promised to take me shopping for new school clothes, and when I got there he made me help him clean the house instead!" Oh, what a flock of tongue-lashing remarks jump into your mouth! It would feel so good to respond with something like "He never could keep his word," or "All he thinks women are good for is cleaning," or "The cheap louse just didn't want to spend his money on you." *Don't do it.* Responsible parenting is not a game, so don't be drawn into the play. Instead, an appropriate response would be "I know that changed schedules can be frustrating, but I think it's nice that you and your dad spent the day together. It's clear that the change of plans bothers you, though, so maybe you should talk to him about it." Remember, even if your ex-spouse's consistent "broken promises" broke up your marriage, and still affect your life and that of your kids, that's no longer *your* problem to fix. Your responsibility now lies in setting a good example for your child by following through with your promises and not acting like a "rescuing" parent. It's a wonderful opportunity to teach your children how to effectively solve problems, to negotiate, and to compromise.

It's not always easy to avoid taking on the rescuing role. Take, for instance, Joe and Susan and their two daughters (from Chapter 3). Susan's life is devoted to being a good parent, and she works very hard at it. Right now their 16-year-old daughter, Lynn, is dating a young man that both Joe and Susan feel is "too old" for her. "This guy she's dating," Susan says, "he's really been a problem. Joe would like her not to be dating him, but . . . so would I (*laughs*). But she's going to see him now." When asked if Lynn discussed her boyfriend with her mother, Susan responded, "Oh, yes, she does at times. We don't get into

73

in-depth conversation about him. I would prefer that she talk about it with her therapist, honestly, you know. I'm much happier if she talks to him, because he's going to be more objective than I am. I'm going to be looking at 'my little girl,' you know. I can't help that, but he's going to be looking at her as a person. A separate entity. And he's going to be more constructive than I am."

Susan and Lynn are making a common mistake in their expectations of what a counselor can do. A good counselor is not expected to be an "objective third party." The role of the therapist-counselor should be to work with the entire family together to teach the members how to discuss these issues openly and honestly. Even if both parents won't participate, at least Susan (Mom) and Lynn (daughter) should be receiving "counsel" about having these talks.

When Susan sends Lynn off to the counselor to discuss these issues, she's giving some implicit messages. The first message Susan is giving is "I can't solve these problems myself. I'm incompetent." Both Susan and Lynn come to believe this. The next implicit message is that "this is Lynn's problem" so we have to send her off to "fix it" with the counselor. Mom and Dad are saying, "It's not my problem." Yet another implicit message being given here is that something is wrong or sick *with Lynn.* This builds resentment on her part, because she feels that it's not *her* problem. If *she* had a problem with it, she wouldn't be dating this guy in the first place. The problem is with Mom and Dad, as it relates to Lynn's behavior.

Susan says that the girls' father, Joe, often disappoints the children by promising things he doesn't come through with, or by being several hours late for parenting time, or by not showing up at all. Susan says, "If it's a minor thing, I'll say, 'OK, next time,' or whatever, but if it's something much more important, that they were really planning on and they're really disappointed, I'll say, 'Yeah, he's kind of self-centered, and he gets involved in different things and everything else comes second. Well, something must have come up that he felt was more important,' and they will come to understand that they're not a priority, which is really true. You know, Joe is the only priority in Joe's life, and everything else is secondary."

By responding like this, Susan is intervening in the relationship between her children and their father, setting up a "sideline instigator" game. If their complaints to Susan persist, and she feels her children find the problem more than they can handle, she could suggest the whole family talk with a counselor, just as she could have done when the problem was her daughter's boyfriend. This counselor should be a professional, not a family friend or an aunt or uncle, because these issues are very complex and some expertise is needed. Well-meaning attitudes are not a substitute for skilled counseling.

Once counseling has begun, there may still be questions, but the family can discuss them and focus on a mutually acceptable solution. Remember, each person needs permission to work out the disagreement with the other parent or family member, even if it is uncomfortable. Children want and need to have the freedom to have a relationship with each parent, separate from the other.

Sometimes, especially with young children, a problem between the children and a noncustodial parent is created when there has been a long separation. The children may be afraid of the upcoming time together. In this case, encourage them to express their fears. Often they don't know why they're afraid, and getting them to talk will help them manage their anxieties. For instance, a young child (ten years or younger) may be going by train to visit the other parent who lives in another state. You can begin getting your child to relax by creating a silly imagined situation. You might ask your child, "Are you afraid that the train might fly off into the sky?" Chances are the child will laugh at the absurdity of a train flying off into the sky, and that can encourage the child to talk about his or her real fears. Then you can address those issues. The point here is to avoid jumping to the conclusion that your child needs you more than he or she needs the other parent, and therefore should stay home with you, to avoid "upsetting the child."

The "martyr game" is another competition tactic favored by divorced parents. In this game, one parent keeps control over the child by making the child feel inappropriately responsible for that parent's "suffering," because the child has positive feelings for the other parent. Strategies in this case include sulking, brooding, faraway looks, attitudes of apparent unselfishness, and performances depicting overwhelming hurt. The martyr seeks to make the child feel guilty for any feelings that conflict with the martyr's emotions and wishes.

The historical role of the martyr was to voluntarily suffer a painful death or sacrifice his or her position for the sake of principle (usually religious). But the modern martyr is only committed to his or her own self-interests and accumulation of pity by inflicting guilt on those who care about the martyr. Note that the victim must *care* about the instigator enough to succumb to the guilt feelings. Without the element of "caring," the process just doesn't work. Because children have such a need to care about their parents, they are easy victims.

A behavioral psychologist might say that the principles of negative reinforcement are at play in the game of martyrdom. First a negative stimulus—"You're hurting me"—is presented. When the person directly or indirectly accused of doing the hurting (the child) displays the correct behavior (or stops the undesired one), the negative stimulus is removed. This reinforces the behavior that gets rid of the negative stimulus. In other words, the parent says, in essence, "You're hurting me." The child answers,

"Oh. I'm sorry. I'll do what you want." The parent responds, "You're a wonderful child. Thank you for not hurting me anymore."

This simple ploy of manipulation is quite effective in getting short-term behavior change, but the long-term effects can be devastating for the child and unproductive for the parent. Rats learn very early that the best way to avoid a negative stimulus is to avoid the situation altogether. This means that if a parent is playing "martyr" and thus using guilt as a negative reinforcer, then the best way for the child to avoid this unpleasant situation is to avoid the parent. Many children learn to do just that, once they become adults, which is why the long-term effects are unproductive for the parent. Unfortunately, the short-term effects can be so gratifying to the "martyr parent" that, unless he or she changes this destructive behavior, the children may internalize the guilt (that is, learn guilt behavior themselves) and learn to be martyrs themselves.

A psychology major in undergraduate school, Janice was a master at playing "martyr parent." Her children were just 3 and 6 years old when she and their father, Jack, divorced. Jack made it a priority in his life to maintain contact with the children, and at first the children responded positively to his presence in their lives. However, Janice was extremely bitter about the divorce and decided that if Jack didn't want her, he couldn't have the children either. She began her strategy by setting up the scenario with the children that it was she and them against the world. When Jack began living with another woman, Janice explained to the children that "Now Daddy has Arlene, and I have you." She constantly reminded the children that she was very lonely and that they were her only source of fun and love. Whenever the children returned from spending time with their father, she moped around the house as though she'd lost her best friend. The happier the children seemed from having seen their father, the more depressed she acted. The children quickly learned that, if they didn't want to hurt Mom's feelings, they'd better not show that they'd had a good time with Dad. Sure enough, if they returned home *complaining* about something that hadn't gone the way they'd wanted it to, they were welcomed, not by the sad, brooding parent who usually faced them on their return, but by a warm, consoling mother who quickly became playful, giddy, and eager to entertain them.

It wasn't long before the children actually began to create unpleasant situations when they were with their father, to calm the mental conflict and guilt they felt, which was brought about by their mother's behavior. People need agreement in their lives between what they know and how they behave. If there's an inconsistency, they'll either change their perception of the facts, or they'll change their behavior to create harmony. In this case, the children were expected to act as if they'd had a bad time with their father, and so they tried to fulfill that expectation. Although the children could have chosen to have a good time with their father, and to display that good time to their mother, they saw her as a fragile parent who needed their love and support, while they perceived their father as a self-sufficient adult who could get along without them. Remember, their father had Arlene, but all their mother had was them.

When a parent is anxious or depressed, quite often the children feel responsible and wonder what they did wrong. In this case, they didn't even have to wonder. Their mother, by playing the "martyr parent," let them know exactly what they did wrong ("You enjoyed your father's company"), and showed them how they could fix it ("Don't enjoy spending time with your father").

Many martyr parents would have stopped here, but not Janice. Once she had the children complaining on a fairly consistent basis about the time they spent with their father, she then began using the same tactics to dissuade them from seeing him altogether. Whenever they said, "Daddy called to see us. Can we go?" she'd respond with a dejected, hurting voice, "Well, do you *want* to go?" If they said yes, even with reservations, she'd say, "Well, I guess so," well up with tears, and disappear into her bedroom. Again, the children learned to give into her wishes by saying, "No, we don't want to go," even though they missed their father very much and enjoyed being with him. Within a few years, the children had cut off all contact with their dad, refusing even to talk with him on the phone. Of course, Janice's perception was that the children just didn't want to see their dad, and that she just hated to "make them" do it.

The most important skill employed in the "martyr parent" game is to persistently imply to your child that "if you love me, you'll do what makes me happy." The underlying message conveyed is that to love the other parent is to destroy you. There are many guilt-inducing comments that can be used, but the good players are sure to pepper these remarks with plenty of sad looks and sighs. Although the object of the game is to destroy the relationship between your children and their other parent, a secondary goal of the "martyr parent" game is that your children will take on the responsibility for *your* happiness.

For instance, Amelia is a 20-year-old who has taken on the responsibility for her mother's happiness. When Amelia was 11 years old, she moved out of her mother's home and went to live with her father, Jeff, and her step-mother, Claudia. Jeff says, "Amelia's mother went crazy. She screamed at her [11-year-old Amelia] on the phone, 'How dare you leave me?' and 'You're a rotten child,' and 'You're breaking my heart,' and 'How am I going to live without you?' Our daughter simply held the phone out . . . she didn't want to hear it . . . she just held the phone out. But it took its toll later. About two or three years later, our daughter really felt like shit. She felt very guilty about leaving her mother. That's when we ran into some very serious problems with her."

Amelia's stepmother, Claudia, says, "Amelia's mother has never let up. To this day she writes to Amelia, 'I can't believe you ever left me, not now, and not when you were 11. I cry when you leave as I cried when you left, every time you've left for the past years and years.'" Claudia continues, "She [the mother] hasn't let up. She's never let up. I mean, she just works that kid over. And then Amelia cries and gets on the phone and sobs and says, 'I'm sorry. I didn't mean to hurt you.' Now, at 20, Amelia's going to go home. She's going to go and make things all right. It's awful."

"Amelia's mother is a lonely woman," says Jeff, "so she's told Amelia that *she* is her friend. In fact, she told her, 'You're my best friend.' I don't think she [the mother] has any friends, so in a sense she's being honest. Amelia is her only friend. It's awful. It's so crippling. It's so bad. Poor Amelia! She's caught in this. It's like a pinball machine. She's the ball. She's among the flippers. She's bounced all over the place. She doesn't know how to establish relationships with parents."

Amelia's mother is clearly an expert player at "martyr parent." She uses emotional bullying with phrases, including "You've left me," "I'm lonely," "I cry every morning," and "I can't believe you're not here."

Although this strategy is far less subtle than that used by Janice in the last example, noncustodial parents are often more aggressive in their play, because they have less access to their children. Their persistence unfortunately pays off in the short term, as in this case where 20-year-old Amelia is quitting college to move back in with her mother.

Amelia's stepmother is concerned about Amelia's apparent need to placate her mother by moving in with her.

In an attempt to encourage her stepdaughter to consider some other alternatives, she said to her, "Imagine, Amelia, that you said to both your mother and your dad, 'Listen, you two. I'm transferring to Oxford. To heck with you. I'm off.' How do you think they'd react?"

After thinking for a while, Amelia responded, "Mother would weep and cry and worry about me. But I guess my dad would really like that. He'd be proud of me. He wants me to be independent. But I just couldn't do that to my mom."

A 20-year-old ought to be able to do that. She wouldn't be doing it *to* her mother. But Amelia is trying to recapture what she thought she might have had, had she stayed with her mother when she was 11. Her stepmother tried to explain this concept to her. "I understand, you missed that [living with her mother as an adolescent], and you're sorry you missed it, but you can't get it back. You're 20. This is nine years later, and you can't get it back. Your mother and you are different people. You have to love each other the way you are now." Going home to live in her mommy's house with her mommy to play house and be dependent again isn't what a 20-year-old should be doing. Unfortunately, at this point, Amelia feels so much guilt that she can't see she's a pawn in her mother's desperately destructive game.

If you suspect that your older children are being manipulated by the "martyr parent" game, you can teach them to avoid the trap of guilt without having to leave home or hide out. They can learn to break up the "martyr" communication sequence early in its formation. This is done by addressing the issue directly, rather than being suckered into it by the "If you really cared..." line.

For example, a mother has told her child, "If you really cared about my feelings, you wouldn't spend so much time with your father." The message is that the child spending time with the father will somehow injure the mother. In fact, very little about mother is the responsibility of the child. The proper response to this complaint would be "Mom, when did you first start thinking that I didn't care about your feelings?" This usually stops the ploy and lets the child get on with a more rational conversation. It's important in breaking up the communication sequence to respond literally to the first part of the sentence, rather than the guilt grabber at the end. A proper response to the second part of the sentence is "How much time I spend with Dad is not related to my feelings toward you. How you manage your feelings is not a responsibility of mine, although I am certainly concerned about it."

With younger children, your part is to constantly reassure them of their own value, and remind them that they cannot and do not control the way other people feel. It is also especially important to help them build strong self-esteem. One result of growing up with a martyr parent is that children become self-critical and demeaning of their own accomplishments, so it is imperative to reinforce a good self-image consistently. Be aware of the need for counseling at crucial times. Amelia and her father could have gone to counseling early on, to learn how to avoid what Amelia is experiencing now.

If you are the parent who finds yourself using martyrdom as a way of manipulating your children, learn some new ways of communicating, negotiating, and compromising with others. Martyrdom, remember, is when you find yourself feeling that the sacrifices you are making are unreasonable, or that by making these sacrifices you have somehow earned yourself a favor or better positioned yourself to control others. Manipulation or trying to control others can be very destructive for everyone. If you can make a concession without expecting anything in return, then you are not being a martyr. If you can make concessions with no intention of imposing guilt or directing behavior change on the part of others, then you're not being a martyr. Avoiding the trap of martyrdom requires skillful insight into your own motives for sacrifice—knowing why you are doing this. The ideal situation is not sacrifice but negotiation. Negotiation occurs when the desires of all involved are open and perhaps both sides make concessions to get mutual satisfaction. The alternative to martyrdom is negotiation, compromise, and mutual agreement. Counseling can be a great teaching source for those who wish to improve their talents in negotiation and communication.

In the case of 20-year-old Amelia, which was discussed earlier in this chapter, her father says that he takes partial responsibility for his daughter's guilt feelings even though they are augmented by her mother's guilt-inducing behavior. He says regretfully, "I told my daughter (when she was a child) that if she ever wanted to come and live with my wife and me, I would pursue it. But I didn't want to say she had to, because *I wanted it to be her idea.* What we ended up doing was putting this tremendous burden on her because she bore the responsibility of leaving her mother. *It would have alleviated her guilt if she'd have been able to say it was beyond her control.* She felt as though she was abandoning her mother."

A child should never be placed in a position where he or she has to bear the responsibility of choosing between the parents. And it's a problem, because, on the surface, it sounds like a good thing to let your children make the choice. The child has rights. You're listening to what the child wants to do. But when you're dealing with preadolescent and early adolescent children, it's a terrible mistake. Even when a child expresses his or her preference to live with one parent rather than the other, it's adults who make those decisions. Children shouldn't be led to *think* that they have the power or responsibility to make such monumental judgments. If a parent says, "No, you may not live with me," then the child must abide by that decision. If a judge says,

"No, you may not live with your mother," then the child must abide by that decision. To pretend that the child is in control burdens the child, because the decision-making responsibility can be much too big a burden for a young person.

Amelia has suffered tremendous guilt because she feels she abandoned her mother. Where most teenagers decorate their rooms with pictures of rock stars or sports figures, Amelia adorns her room with photographs of her mother, as though she were creating a shrine. Whenever Amelia visits her mother, she comes back very depressed; pale with grief and red-eyed from weeping. Her step-mother says that Amelia feels the same grief now when she says good-bye to her mother as she did when she was 11 years old. She phones her mother daily, talking to her for forty-five minutes at a time, and then often grieving when the phone call has ended. As a teenager, she became reclusive and uncommunicative at home, partly due to adolescence, but also as a way of getting rid of the anger she felt at having been put into the position of abandon-ing her mother. Then she became angry that she felt guilty, and began to act sullen and nasty. The guilt has prolonged juvenile behavior from her and an unwillingness to become independent. Her mother's need to control Amelia's life has infantilized her.

Amelia's sense of self has also taken a real pounding. She seems riddled with insecurity and uprootedness. She doesn't have much confidence in her ability to strive and succeed at anything. Her choices in boyfriends reflect her low regard for herself. "And it's sad," her stepmother says, with real affection for Amelia. "Both parents obviously have adored her and fought over her and longed for her, and they still compete for her. I'm not quite sure why that doesn't translate into an extreme sense of value—not *de*value. I don't know how she got so diminished."

It's easy to get so involved in our pride and need for approval that we seek it from our children, especially if those needs have been unmet during a divorce. We are all capable of getting wrapped up in our own egos, and it's so nice to hear a child say to you, "I don't want to go live with my mother [or father]. I want to live with you." You say to yourself, "See, I'm right. I was right. I won. I got it. I won this." And that's the problem—it's so reward-ing. If the noncustodial parent is being chosen, that also absolves him or her from the social stigma attached to "los-ing custody of your child." And it's so punishing for the other parent, and that, sadly, can become another re-inforcement. Meanwhile, the children become the buffers, forced to take on decision-making responsibilities that will lead to questions of loyalty and guilt.

By defaulting on parental responsibility—by giving the child power to make the decision about where he or she will live, another destructive potential is created: the "You made your bed, now lie in it" game. This game is marked by parental phrases such as "I don't understand what's the matter with you. You *wanted* to live here. *You* decided to live here. *You* came to live with us." Suddenly the children feel trapped by what they may now perceive to be their bad decision, and that begins to undermine the confidence they have in their ability to make good decisions.

Dumping the responsibility of decision making onto the child doesn't have to involve the choice of where the child will live, to be destructive. In the following case, for instance, the choice of noncustodial parent access was left up to the children. The behavior demonstrated by the father in the case is not appropriate. It shows a wide range of tactics that can cripple children. And chances are it will also demonstrate that your own situation probably could be worse.

Bruce was in his late twenties when he and his wife, Laurie, were divorced. Because of Laurie's inability to care for the children financially, Bruce was given custody of them, and she was given liberal access. The access Laurie was awarded was also flexible so that she could return to school and prepare herself for financial self-sufficiency.

Bruce could not accept the fact that Laurie didn't want to be married to him any longer. He decided there must be something mentally wrong with her for her to have left him, and so it was his duty to protect the children from her. Yet he was faced with a court decree that gave her liberal access. He decided the best way to solve his dilemma was for the children to "decide" that they didn't want to see her anymore.

The first thing he did was to begin denying Laurie access. The less the children saw of their mother, he felt, the more impact his presence and attitudes would have on them. Also, with minimal contact between the children and Laurie, Bruce could reinforce the children's feelings of abandonment by their mother. He began using excuses for turning down her requests for parenting time that included "unofficial holidays" such as Pancake Day (we have pancakes together every Saturday) and Family Day (Sundays are for families, and you are no longer part of our family). He wrote to Laurie's family members that "I have a family. Laurie chose to no longer be a part of it. You are no longer a part of it." He would play "bait and switch," promising Laurie that she could see the children, but then on the scheduled day he would pretend that he had forgotten and would tell the children he'd made plans to take them to the amusement park. He would deny Laurie access, telling her that he and the children had other plans, and then tell the children she was coming. When she didn't arrive, he would phone her in front of the children and act upset, saying things such as "The children made you a special dinner. Where are you? How can you let them down like this?"

When Laurie disciplined the children while they were in her custody, Bruce withdrew access from her completely, telling the children he would protect them from her ("rescuing parent"). He would grant Laurie access, and then be gone with the children when she arrived to pick them up. Once he remarried, he told the children that his new wife was now "Mother," and that they were not to refer to Laurie as "Mother" any longer. When Laurie finally told Bruce that she would take him back to court if he didn't stop interfering with her parenting time with the children, he told them, "Laurie is taking *us* [*he* and *the children*] back to court again." Bruce also threatened her that, if she sued him, he would make sure that by the time the case went to court the children would never want to see her again.

And by the time the case went to court, he no longer had to deny Laurie access. The children were now convinced that there was something wrong with their mother, as expressed by 10-year-old Melissa when she reported to the judge, referring to her mother's attempts at access, "It's like she bugs us a lot." Bruce used their refusal to spend time with their mother as a proof of their love for him, getting them to repeat over and over again that they didn't want to see Laurie.

Bruce was also an expert at playing "martyr parent." The children were convinced that Laurie had done something unpardonable when she divorced Bruce. Twelve-year-old Ryan expressed it clearly when he told the judge, "I could never forgive her for walking out on my dad."

Although the case of Bruce and Laurie may seem extreme by normal standards, this kind of game playing takes place in homes across the world every day. The tragedy is that there are no real winners in these games, but there are losers. *The losers are our children.*

When children are called on to take sides with one parent against another, they can't win. If they side with the custodial parent, or the parent they perceive to be the master of the situation, they feel guilty about turning their backs on the weaker parent. If they side with the non-custodial parent, or the parent they perceive to be in the weaker position, then they lose by association. For the children, it is a no-win situation, and they are the losers.

In most of the psychological games parents play, the initiators are fighting for control. The game becomes a competition for authority and power over the other parent, and over the children as well. One of the most difficult aspects of dealing with this behavior is that the initiating parent is usually convinced that his or her actions are "right" and that anyone with an opposing view is "wrong." If you are one of these self-righteous parents, you are not alone.

Self-righteousness seems to be a common condition among the human race. We seem to have a need to be right. Receiving custody of children can seem to reaffirm these feelings of being right. It can bolster the belief that we *deserve* the authority and control over our children and over the other parent, because the courts have given us that power. We perceive the legal system as an ally and its decision as confirmation that the custodial parent is the "good" parent, and that the other parent is therefore the "bad" parent. Particularly if the other parent has initiated an unwanted divorce, a feeling of self-righteousness can envelop us. If we don't recognize and overcome that feeling, it can lead us into destructive behavior.

But losing custody can also bring on self-righteous behavior. Even if we are not asking for custody, granting it to the other parent can make us feel like "losers." It can perpetuate feelings of self-doubt and inadequacy, which can lead to a need to vindicate ourselves in our own eyes, as well as in the eyes of society. When custody is given to the other parent, and is therefore taken away from us, society tends to view that as a statement on our parenting skills. It is not uncommon for the noncustodial parent to be considered as inadequate or deficient. In an effort to exonerate ourselves, and to prove how wrong the other parent really is, self-righteousness can be used as our rationale to fight for control.

In overcoming self-righteousness, first you have to recognize it. When you're involved in a disagreement with your former spouse about a particular issue, ask yourself

- Do I care more about the issue, or more about who has the power to make the decision?

- Do I care more about the issue, or more about proving my authority?

- Do I care more about the issue, or more about being right?

- Do I care more about the issue, or more about proving that my former spouse is wrong?

- Am I really listening to my former spouse, or am I so sure that I'm right that I'm refusing to listen?

- Am I so sure that I'm right that I refuse to give in, even when my former spouse makes a good point?

Self-righteousness can be destructive. If you recognize it in yourself, you need to face the reality that no one is always right. Recognize that we all have our own viewpoints and that each of us can be right from his or her own perspective. Multiple realities do exist, and to deny this ensures our own emotional immaturity. Our children will not be hurt from exposure to different points of view. The damage comes from the parent who is so insistent on proving his or her "rightness" that he or she plays psychological games where the stakes are the children themselves.

If, after going through the set of questions just given, you find that you truly are angry with your former spouse about a specific issue, then confront him or her about the issue, setting an appropriate time and place (as discussed in Chapter 3). Provide ample time and opportunity for your ex-spouse to state his or her case. Don't confuse your unhappiness about the relationship with your former spouse (for example, being divorced) with the issue itself. You're not going to solve anything by spewing out unrelated hostility. Also, recognize that discussing a specific issue with your former spouse does not guarantee that the issue will be resolved. This should not stop you from expressing your concerns, but be sure to clarify the issue. First, you can test the waters to see if your former spouse is even open to discussing the problem. For instance, an exchange might go like this:

A: I have a problem with your always being late to pick up the kids. Is this a good time to discuss it?
B: Yes.
A: Fine.
or
A: I have a problem with your always being late to pick up the kids. Is this a good time to discuss it?
B: No.
A: Then when? Let's schedule a time right now.

If the response to that is "There is no good time," then at least you know where your former spouse stands on the issue. It may be your former spouse's method of continuing the fight. It may not be fair. But it's the way it is. Remember, you *can't* change anyone else's behavior. You *can* change your own.

You can always seek legal recourse, but chances are that "being late" is not a significant enough issue to go to court. A better solution is to set a time limit: "I will wait twenty minutes. After that, I will have to make other

90

plans." In this method, you are changing your behavior, over which you have control.

In summary, learn to recognize if you are a player in any of these devastating interactions. It's amazing how, as adults, we cling to those old, unproductive, childish games. You would think that we could learn new and more effective ways of communicating . . . and we can. First, it takes a conscious desire to stop the old, manipulative ways of managing our loved ones. Then, it takes a true desire to become a "student," open to learning. If you are the one initiating the games, take the suggestions in this chapter to learn new ways of communicating and interacting with others. If you are one of the unwitting players, we have suggested methods in this chapter to get out of the game. Remember, these games create no-win situations in which our children are the losers.

▼
Chapter
5

Situational Peace

The development of psychoanalysis by Sigmund Freud in 1896 introduced the idea that, by some sort of "working through" process, people could be relieved of emotional discomfort and suffering. Although long-term therapy (psychoanalysis or any one of dozens of other therapies) may be beneficial for the few who can afford it, it has become more trendy than practical. That is not to say that it's bad, or even unrewarding, to work on digging up your resentments toward your former spouse. Working through your resentments can be a very healthy, rewarding experience for you, but it's also something that can take years of expensive therapy and hard work to accomplish. Also, there is no guarantee that it will ever work. Your child cannot be put on hold while you experiment. Your child needs you *now*, whether you're "over the divorce" or not. Your child's needs must be met now, no matter what your "inner feelings" are concerning your former marriage partner. Your children don't have time for your self-actualization to proceed until everything is resolved. The bitter conflict between you and your former spouse does not have to be resolved in order for you to behave in a civil and appropriate manner toward your child's other parent.

It's fine to seek therapy or counseling, but in the meantime you must behave suitably. You may *feel* better after two years in therapy, or five years, or ten years, but how you *act* now will have a lasting effect on your children.

For most of us, the "therapeutic trick" to adjustment is to make peace with a specific set of circumstances, rather than to somehow solve all emotional problems simultaneously. Psychoanalytic theory assumes that behavior is a symptom of some deep underlying cause. The theory further asserts that the way to change behavior or feelings is to root out this cause through psychoanalysis; the resulting insight is supposed to let you feel and act differently.

Behavioral approaches, in contrast, seek to modify behavior so as to adapt or fit the circumstances presented. Over the past forty years, there has been much debate, and indeed conflict, between the behavioral approach and the psychoanalytic approach to therapy. Which should come first: (1) resolution of the underlying problems deep in the unconscious, which changes feelings and behavior; or (2) a behavior change that, as a first success, lets the individual manage immediate situations more effectively? Some experts argue that the behavior change gives insight into the underlying causes (this argument is an attempt to marry behaviorism and psychoanalysis). Through modifying behavior, it is possible, although not necessary, that these underlying causes will be resolved.

In the case of conflicts with ex-spouses, or indeed with anyone with whom we need or want to interact, making peace with the situation offers immediate benefit and does not require long-term therapy. For example, a few years ago an elderly man was asked how he and his wife maintained such a successful marriage. He responded, "She stays upstairs, and I stay downstairs." This is a good example of situational peace.

"Not the best solution to the problem," you say? "What about talking through the conflict?" you ask. "What about better communication? What about working through the problems?" For those of you who ask these questions, try to understand how much influence the past 90-odd years of the "Therapy Era" have had on our lives. From a practical point of view, the elderly man and his wife, when presented with a number of conflicts, decided to handle the situation by defining home territory as safe ground. By occupying their safe ground (she upstairs and he downstairs), they could choose their time and place to be together while maintaining their respective and needed privacy. They had achieved *situational peace,* which allowed them to live their lives in a mutually comfortable manner. Although this is not to suggest that all married couples should follow their pattern, who are we to condemn their solution? In fact, their approach offers the divorced parent a good example of situational peace achieved between emotionally attached individuals.

Children need to have both parents participate in the important events in their lives, and parents need to enjoy situational peace during these occasions. Often these events cannot be postponed until you "feel" ready to face them. These occasions include recitals, important sports events, graduations, first communions, confirmations, bar and bat mitzvahs, weddings, and even funerals. Regardless of how you feel about your former spouse, it is important that when you attend these activities, you act civilly and politely toward your child's other parent and his or her family. Many parents attend these functions with tied up, knotted stomachs, and clenched fists. Parents face these events every day, but seldom with any sense of comfort or peace. This chapter is intended to give you direction in creating situational peace during these events, so that both you and your children will enjoy the time and have happy memories of these momentous occasions.

Situational peace can be created even under the most adverse circumstances. Judy and Samuel were in the middle of a major court battle when it was time for their son, David, to be bar mitzvahed. Also, David knew that he must soon leave his mother and go live with his father, Sam, and Sam's new wife, Deborah, if he was to inherit his father's fortune. It should be noted here that the fortune was immense, and even at 12 years old David was aware of what the money could mean to his future. Sam believed that only boys were important, and that girls were less important, so he was perfectly satisfied to leave his daughter in her mother's custody. The child he wanted was David.

Judy was angry with Sam for a lot of reasons. She despised his attitude that women were only meant to keep house for men, and to have dinner on the table for them whenever they returned home. She was bitter about the way this translated into an obvious and overt preference by Sam for David over their daughter. She resented that Sam used his money to influence David's decisions. She was also frustrated by the fact that, in spite of his vast wealth, Sam was often late with child support payments, and even quit paying altogether until she was forced to take him to court. These were the circumstances as they existed when it came time for David's bar mitzvah; hardly a conducive situation for a pleasant time.

However, Judy made up her mind that her negative feelings for Sam would not interfere with the celebration of her son's bar mitzvah. She practiced the concept of focusing on David for the upcoming event, rather than on Sam's negative qualities or behavior. She didn't pretend that Sam wouldn't be present, but she centered her thoughts on her own joy over David's celebration.

The day of the affair arrived. The guest list was made up primarily of Sam's family and friends. The reception was held in an elaborate ballroom; money was no object.

It might have been all very intimidating to Judy, had she not been prepared for the situation, but as it was she felt in complete control of herself and her emotions. It was even Judy's idea that both she and Sam walk in together with their son when he was introduced to the guests at the reception, so as his name was announced he appeared with his mother on one arm and his father on the other. Judy says it was the way David wanted it, and by creating situational peace for herself she was able to enjoy the honor with genuine pleasure.

Most of the challenges in our lives require us to adapt to situations presented to us by life. Those of us who are flexible adapt more easily and suffer much less long-term anxiety and emotional trauma about those changes in our world. The more skilled we become at managing change, the more flexible we can become, and thus more likely to achieve situational peace in our lives.

Being flexible and adapting to change are not skills we are born with, although some of us come by them more readily than others. Adults who manage change well most likely had parents and home lives that modeled and taught change as a way of life. For those of us who didn't have that "natural" education, it is comforting to know that it's never too late to learn.

Learning new skills is a matter of practice. To gain a new talent, you must repeat the new behavior often, and in the right context. Fortunately, our minds have an amazing capacity to sort out the mistakes we make in developing new skills, so don't be afraid of temporary setbacks. If you repeat a course of action often enough, it will become the behavior of habit, and soon enough will seem to come "naturally," as if it's second nature. Take, for instance, learning a new sport such as tennis. No amount of theory in the world will let you hit the ball over the net without the experience of physically hitting the ball with the racquet. At first, you will make far more errors than successful shots, but your mind will be able to differentiate between the fewer successful shots and the more frequent errors, and will create a template or pattern for success. This will let you constantly improve your skills, even though initially you may repeat the same mistakes often.

So it is with learning to be more flexible and handling change.

EXERCISE

Flexibility

Pick a daily routine that you have learned, and change it. For example, most of us have become comfortable with the way we put on our clothes. We all have a preferred sequence of dressing. You may put on your left sock before the right, or vice versa. You may put your shirt or blouse on before your skirt or slacks. You may put on your right pants leg before the left, or may button your clothing from top to bottom, or from bottom to top. To practice adapting to flexibility, change the way you dress each time. If you normally put your right arm into its sleeve first, try putting your left arm in first. Whatever your routine is, do it in reverse order. You'll find this a bit uncomfortable at first, and it will take concentration because it is not your preferred order. However, by practicing changing the order, you're conditioning yourself to accept change and to be more comfortable with it. Try this technique with other daily routines as well, such as bathing or showering, brushing your teeth, the order of eating your breakfast, and so on. Take a different route to work or a different mode of transportation. Remember, there are no mistakes, just changes. It seems that the more we need change, the less apt we are to seek it. If you can learn to accept that change is not right or wrong, just different and inevitable, then you can begin to engineer situational peace.

It is important to note that change *doesn't* have to feel good in order for you to do it. "If it feels good, do it," is a phrase that's been with us since the 1960s. At that time in our culture, when our own sense of satisfaction with a situation or set of circumstances determined how we would behave, we built some self-centeredness into our lives. Not that looking out for ourselves is wrong—but in reality, if we all waited for something to "feel good" before we did it, very little would ever get done.

More recently our culture has adopted a "no pain, no gain" attitude toward physical fitness. Perhaps we should also breed this stance into our mental fitness program as well. If we were to do so, how might that affect our behavior?

Treating a former spouse with respect may not always "feel good," but so what? Negative feelings about doing something, or while doing something, should not become a reason for not doing it. Unfortunately, our culture is still caught in the "If it feels good, do it" rationale. If someone tells us that they don't feel good about doing something, we are apt to respond with "Oh, OK. If it doesn't feel good, we wouldn't want you to do it." This is absurd. The premise assumes that any behavior that is uncomfortable should be avoided. Remember, it's OK to be uncomfortable. After all, you taught your children to behave in situations where they had to share with someone they didn't particularly like. And, presumably, we want them to learn to make ethically correct choices, even when the less ethical choice seems easier. If they can do it, you can do it.

It is not necessary to repress negative feelings toward a former spouse in order to enjoy situational peace. On the contrary, it can be very unhealthy to stuff thoughts and feelings into the unconscious when unresolved conflicts still exist. When emotions are repressed, they can affect the health and actions of an individual without that person even being aware of the cause of his or her condition or behavior. Emotional issues need to be looked at and dealt with. However, feelings need not be repressed in order to be occasionally put on hold until an appropriate time and place presents itself. Then those feelings can be investigated and, at some point, resolved.

The notion that we may have to wait for something we want is an unfamiliar concept in our fast-paced culture. Especially in our cities today, it has become commonplace to feast on fast foods, buy clothing off the racks, obtain instant money, receive instant credit, and demand instant answers. The same is becoming true of our emotions. If we are hurt, angered, or frustrated, we are being taught that we should not "hold it inside" but should "get it out into the open." Consistent with our fast food culture, we are becoming a "fast feel culture," where everything needs to be done and said right now; dumping our emotions is encouraged.

You do not have to act on your emotions as you feel them. It is perfectly rational for you to consciously choose to postpone the release of your feelings until a time when their release will not hurt others. Because family occasions of celebration take place in a very finite time, the duration of your emotional postponement has known, defined boundaries that can make the experience more predictable. The clue to achieving situational peace, then, is to intentionally expel your negative emotions from your consciousness for the interval of the event or occasion that you are attending.

You can do this by directing your energies into your child. Concentrate on the event itself, and on your child's enjoyment of the occasion. After all, that is why you are there. You are not there to see how your ex-spouse behaves. It is not a wise idea to try and steal glances, or to pay attention to whom he or she speaks or doesn't. Your ex-spouse's

clothes have no relevance to you, nor does his or her decision to bring along a companion.

Although it may seem to you unsympathetic for your
former marriage partner to "flaunt" his or her significant
(or insignificant) other in front of you, it is not your
business. It is your job to be prepared for the possibility,
and to be in enough control to postpone releasing your
feelings until after the celebration. If the likelihood causes
you anxiety, prepare for it using the neurosemantic exercises from Chapter 3. Remember, your children will be
watching you to see how you react. If you behave politely
and civilly under these conditions, it may help them to
do the same if they are upset by the presence of the new
companion. Remember, loyalty to you is a likely reason
your children might take offense at the presence of a new
person in your former spouse's life, and anything you can
do to relieve your children of these loyalty and guilt feelings will add to their pleasure in the festivities.

It is helpful in developing situational peace to remember Shakespeare when he referred to the world as but "a
stage, where every man must play a part" (*Merchant of Venice*,
Act I, Sc. 1). It is almost as though he were describing the
situation in which we divorced parents find ourselves,
because in coparenting it doesn't matter what we think
of the other parent. It only matters how we act. We've all
had experience acting, whether it was dramatic acting or
social acting. We've all been called on to use our skills con-
vincingly to project a certain image. In our everyday lives,
we act out different roles, depending on the situation.
Most of us project differently toward our children (confident, self-assured) from the way we act toward our parents
(subordinate, trying to please). We act differently in front
of our bosses (flexible) from the way we act in front of
our staff (firm). We put up with behavior from our friends
that we would never tolerate from our marriage partners.

We've all been in situations where we've had to behave nicely and politely even though we were uncomfortable doing it. We may have wanted to get up and leave or to speak our minds, but instead we had to sit there and endure it. We used our skills in social acting to get through the occasion.

As with any skill, proficiency in social acting improves and sharpens with practice, until it becomes second nature. Here are some exercises you can practice to help you keep focused on your role of "parent," rather than on that of "ex-spouse."

EXERCISE

Muscle Association

In acting, *walking* through a part increases your ability to memorize lines, because physical movement can act as a mental stimulus. So it is helpful to practice small physical changes in preparing to share an event with your child's other parent.

For example, nervous hands are usually a dead give-away to a person's state of mind. Controlling your hand movements can help you focus on your parent "role," as well as help you project an image of confidence.

When a woman is seated, her hands should be positioned, one on top of the other, on her lap in a relaxed manner. She may hold them both palms up, both palms down, or the palm of the bottom hand up with the top hand palm down. Her elbows should be touching her sides, and her shoulders should be relaxed.

When a man is seated, his hands should not be clasped together, but should be relaxed and still. He can put one or both in his pockets, place one on each knee, or perhaps one or both on his hips.

These positions are about the same when you are standing. For women, the hands are clasped in front of you, or held down at your sides. For men, keep your hands in your pockets, or down at your sides. The point is to keep them still and in control.

As you practice this exercise, associate it in your mind with controlling your focus of attention. Think about pouring your energies into your child and focusing your attention on the activities of the day.

When preparing to give or attend a social function, it is always helpful to know the right thing to do at the right time. In today's society, where divorce has become common, proper etiquette has shriveled into a back-pedaling mishmash. The reason most often given for this hesitancy to set guidelines for social behavior between divorced people is that it has been considered acceptable for divorced couples to behave badly toward one another. We do not accept the premise that divorced people should be excluded from the requirements of good manners.

Good manners basically boil down to a saying of the ancient world: "Do *not* do to others what you do *not* want done to you." Christians thought so much of the concept that it was incorporated (in a positive form) into the New Testament. Good manners help create a situation in which people treat each other with civility and politeness. In an atmosphere based on such principles, children and adults alike can more easily find situational peace.

When faced with a social event to be shared with a former spouse, consider the behavior of diplomats. Diplomats have used rules of protocol in their ceremonies and diplomatic exchanges throughout history. These rules of decorum are designed to help rivals meet easily and to avoid direct confrontations. Their behavior is very civil and careful, with no attempt at any emotional attachment. A good diplomat can gain the respect of others without stimulating passion for his or her cause.

It is much easier for both hosts and guests when there are etiquette guidelines to follow. When people know what to expect, everything can run much more smoothly. Knowing the right thing to do gives people confidence and inspires appropriate and obliging behavior. Here are three major guidelines:

1. Include the other parent.
2. Focus on the children at events honoring them.
3. Being polite is always the correct behavior.

The Golden Rule of Etiquette when planning for a special occasion for your child, such as a wedding or a bar or bat mitzvah, is to *include the other parent.* Do not put conditions on his or her appearance, such as "If you come, you must

1. "Pay for the affair."
2. "Pay for half of the affair."
3. "Come alone."
4. "Leave immediately after the temple or church service."
5. "Be excluded from parental traditions."

Although the concept of including the other parent in a celebration for your child may seem self-evident to you, according to many divorced parents it is not. Take, for example, Matthew and Rebecca. Both are well educated. At the time of their divorce, which was thirteen years ago, their sons were 12, 10, and 7. Rebecca was awarded custody and child support. She also had a good income from her position in research and from a family trust.

Matthew talks about his sons' bar mitzvahs. "My three sons were all bar mitzvahed after I left my first wife [Rebecca], and I was not invited to any of the celebrations. My oldest son was bar mitzvahed relatively soon after I left, and I went to the temple with my father and my sister.

It was terrible. It was just terrible. My father was an elderly man, and he broke down and cried. My sister and my (ex-) wife got into an argument. Then I had to leave right after the service. We were not asked to stay, and I was not a part of the party itself.

"By the time it came time for my next son's bar mitzvah, I was living with my present wife, but we were not yet married. I went to the temple by myself, and then left after the service. This was at the recommendation of my rabbi, you know, that I don't stay away. 'You have to appear for the service,' he said, 'because your son is going to look down and want to see you there.'

"By the time my third son was bar mitzvahed, you'd think after all this time, you'd think this would not be. I was married to my present wife by this time. The rabbi said, 'You and Wendy go together.' We waited outside until the service began, and then we walked in and sat in the back row. When it was over, we got up and left. You know, the moment we walked in—and my son was up there—we made immediate eye contact. He was looking for us to walk in. He knew I was there. When the service was over, we went immediately out to the car. I got into the car, looked up, and my son was running out the door. He came over, and then had to go back in, so I have not been to any of the bar mitzvahs—the parties. And now my son is getting married, and I was afraid it would be exactly the same."

Under the circumstances, Matthew showed valor, class, and a dignity that his sons will, we hope, emulate. And Rebecca showed petty vindictiveness by excluding the boys' father from their bar mitzvahs. Such an absence of caring for the boys' feelings on such a highly visible occasion can make everyone feel uncomfortable. Rebecca obviously missed the point that the bar mitzvah is a celebration in recognition of the young man, not the mother.

During the bar or bat mitzvah service, the parents usually sit in the front row together (except at Orthodox services where the women sit in the balcony). Divorced parents may choose to have a child or an empty space between them. It is usual to call the parents to come forward for the reading of the Torah. If the parents insist, they can be called up separately.

For Christians, parents do not usually have a role in the service for their child's first communions and confirmations. However, if both parents are involved in the child's religious upbringing, then it is proper that they both attend the services. These important occasions are often followed by a small reception, and again, it is appropriate for both parents to attend.

When planning special occasions, the question of financial responsibility is often a biting issue. The parent who pays child support each month may feel that, since the party is for the child, the money should come out of that budget. The custodial parent may feel that the expense is above and beyond what the child support payments can cover. Common sense and decency, however, which are the basis for etiquette in the first place, dictate that whichever parent is making the plans and decisions for the party pays for it. This way, the affair will be planned to fit into the budget of the host.

If your children complain that they want a more elaborate party than you can afford, this is a good time to teach them about spendable income. Parents, divorced or not, have suddenly become afraid to tell their children, "We can't afford it." If what you can afford is a cake and punch reception, then that is exactly what you should have. It is not relevant if your former spouse could afford to give your child a country club affair, if he or she is not giving the party. What is important is that you invite the other parent to come and share the cake and punch, or whatever your circumstances will allow.

Also, don't forget to invite the grandparents and other relatives from your former spouse's side of the family. The extended family is important to a child's sense of continuity. It is not your responsibility to make sure they accept the invitation, but it is your duty to invite them. It is also appropriate to ask your former spouse if there are other guests whom he or she would like added to the guest list. For these guests, it is proper to ask that your former spouse contribute the per plate charge for these guests when it is a catered affair. If you are the nonhosting parent, it is your responsibility to offer this contribution. It is also your duty to keep this personal guest list to a minimum, and to include only those people whom you think your children would want in attendance.

Traditionally, the father of the bride paid for his daughter's wedding because, once married, the groom assumed all financial responsibilities for the woman for the rest of her life. Today that premise is absurd. In today's society, it is practical and proper for the person hosting the wedding to assume its expenses. Often this means that the mother of the bride bears the financial responsibility of the wedding, because she and her daughter usually plan the wedding the way they want it. When the bride and groom decide to plan their own wedding, then it is proper and practical for them to assume its expenses.

This does not mean that the father of the bride or the parents of the groom should not offer to contribute. The person hosting the affair should not be offended at such an offer, and should at least consider accepting it. However, this offer must come with no strings attached.

When parents put contingencies on financial help for special occasions, that can lead to feelings of animosity. For example, Matthew and Rebecca, the divorced couple referred to earlier, are now involved with their second son's upcoming wedding. This son and his bride planned a lavish affair that turned out to be far more expensive than the young woman's divorced mother could afford. When this came to light, Rebecca—the groom's mother—stepped in and volunteered to pay for half the wedding. Assuming that everything could now be paid for, the bride and her mother completed the details for the wedding.

A few months before the event, Rebecca dropped a bombshell. She let it be known that she was only going to pay for half the wedding *if* her son's father, Matthew, was not invited. That wasn't acceptable to anyone, so she relented and said Matthew could be there, but Wendy, his wife of eight years, couldn't attend.

The blackmail backfired. Not only did Rebecca draw disappointment from her son and resentment from her future daughter-in-law, but the bride's mother was irate. She had invited her own former husband, the bride's father, when the plans were first announced, and was perfectly aware that he would not be contributing financially to the wedding. In fact, he had abandoned the family years before, but he was invited and had accepted. This made it all the more intolerable to the bride's mother that Rebecca would try to exclude her son's father and his family from the affair, and she made it clear that she was not going to let Rebecca control her daughter's wedding.

In spite of his former wife's attempt at excluding him from their son's wedding, Matthew is looking forward to the festivities. "I told the kids," Matthew says, grinning, "'Don't worry about us. Just tell us where you want us, and we'll be there. Tell us where you want us to sit, and we'll sit there. We don't care what table it is. It can be the closest to the kitchen. We don't plan on sitting very long. We'll be dancing all night, anyway.'"

In cases where both parents are vying for the privilege of paying for the affair, the noncustodial parent should acquiesce to the custodial parent's wishes, keeping in mind the guidelines presented here.

It is not proper, nor fair to your child, to get into a "dueling parties" feud. An example was given by a rabbi who had recently officiated at a bar mitzvah where the boy's mother, whom the rabbi described as "financially strained," had held a luncheon after the service in the temple social room. "Halfway through the luncheon," the rabbi said, "a limousine pulled up in front of the temple. The young man's father, who had chosen not to even attend the service, had come to collect his son for the much more elegant party he was hosting, and the young man knew he was required to leave his mother's party to attend the other one." This behavior by the father put the young man in a position of torn loyalties that no child should be forced to face. This is an example of a parent's vengefulness poorly camouflaged as participating in a child's special occasion. The young man's father was not only rude to his son's mother, the guests, and the rabbi, but also hurt his son. Somewhere he'd lost the point of the whole occasion, which was to recognize the religious maturity of his son.

Invitations to a child's affair can be easily handled without slighting either parent or stepparent, while keeping the focus of the celebration on the child, where it belongs. An invitation to a graduation party might read

Together with her parents

Jane Doe

requests the pleasure of your company . . .

or for a wedding, the invitation might read

Together with their parents

Jane Doe

and

John Smith

request the honor of your presence . . .

This simple form alleviates the problems of trying to fairly reflect who paid for what. In today's society, it is not unusual in a wedding situation for everyone to pitch in financially, including the groom's parents and stepparents, as well the bride and groom. It is also not uncommon for the parents to pay for the honeymoon or help with the down payment on a house, while the bride and groom pay for the wedding themselves. This invitation form also avoids a ridiculously long list of names, while still including everyone. It also sets the tone for cooperation and situational peace.

If the guest list is going to include other than close friends, and the child's last name being different from some of the parents' last names may be confusing, then an insert card can be included where appropriate. For example, if Jane Doe's mother and stepfather's last name is Smith, the small insert cards in the invitations going to those on *their* guest list may read

By invitation of

Mr. and Mrs. John Smith

or, if Jane Doe's mother and stepfather have different last names, the insert card may read

By invitation of

Ms. Mary Brown, Jane's mother,

and

Mr. John Smith, Jane's stepfather

The two most important issues to remember in wording the invitations are first, inclusion rather than exclusion, and second, clarity.

In Jewish weddings in both Reform and Conservative Judaism in the United States, it is traditional for the parents to escort their son or daughter down the aisle together. (In Orthodox services, the father escorts his son and the mother, her daughter, symbolizing the separation of the sexes.) In the case of divorced parents, this is still preferred. It is also acceptable for stepparents to be included in the procession, but this decision is left up to the bride and groom.

Referring back to the upcoming marriage of Rebecca and Matthew's son, Rebecca has absolutely refused to escort their son down the aisle with Matthew. She has told Matthew that it is because it would lead everyone to think that there are no problems between them. Twelve years after the divorce, it is still so important to Rebecca that people know she feels hostile toward her former husband that she is unwilling to set aside her animosity for one day for the sake of her son's wedding. What she wanted, instead, was to escort their son down the aisle by herself. This was unacceptable to Matthew, for to him it was treating him as though he were dead. Because no one can force Rebecca to do what she will not do, neither parent will be participating in that tradition. Instead, their son will walk down the aisle with his brother.

In a Christian ceremony, it is tradition that the father of the bride escort his daughter down the aisle. This is true whether or not the parents are divorced. However, when the bride has been close to both her father and stepfather during her growing-up years, she may wish to have them both escort her, one on each side. Because inclusion is always preferable to exclusion, this alternative to tradition can be a nice choice when the two fathers get along.

In Jewish services, as for seating during the ceremony when parents are divorced, if divorced parents are escorting their child down the aisle together then the new spouses and their children are seated with the other guests for the service. However, if the *huppah,* or marriage canopy, under which the bride and groom stand during the ceremony (optional at Reform weddings) is large enough, anyone may stand under it for the service. In Christian services, the bride's mother, and stepfather if her mother is remarried, sits in the front pew on the left side of the

111

church. If she has children who are not included in the wedding party, they sit with the maternal grandparents and aunts and uncles in the second pew. If it is a large family, then the aunts and uncles can be seated in the third pew. After the father has "given away" his daughter, he sits directly behind the maternal relatives with his family. The groom's family follows the same procedure, only on the right side of the church.

Exceptions to this are, again, based on common sense. If the bride is not close to her mother, and the father is paying for the wedding, then he, and his wife if he is remarried, sit in the first pew.

When planning a wedding reception, remember, there are choices. You are never going to please everyone, and someone will always be able to find fault if they look hard enough. The spirit of the wedding reception is to celebrate the joining of the bride and groom as a married couple, and not to flaunt any particular abilities as the perfect host.

Tradition holds at Christian weddings that parents do not sit at the bridal table, whether or not they are still married to each other. This table is reserved for the bride and groom and the bridal party. When there have been no divorces by either set of parents, it is customary to have a parents' table. This joining of the bride's and groom's parents at the parents' table signifies the joining of the families. However, when there has been a divorce among the sets of parents, it makes more sense to have each parent, or each set of parents and stepparents, host a separate table. This in no way signifies a refusal of the bride's and groom's parents to join together. It merely assures everyone a more relaxed atmosphere in which to eat.

At Jewish wedding receptions, while it is traditional to have a family table when there has been no divorce, it has become customary for divorced parents to each host a different table, and for the bride and groom to host a table with the bridesmaids and ushers.

As for the receiving line, only the mothers of the bride and groom used to head up the line at a Christian wedding. The fathers were not even present. Today, the line-up can be flexible, or the reception line can be abandoned. However, if the bride and groom want to include it, and have a preference for the line-up, their wishes should be followed without complaints or hurt feelings. Finding yourself at the end of the line-up is no reflection on your place in their hearts. Your concentration in the receiving line should be centered on welcoming the guests you know and on meeting those you haven't yet been introduced to, and not on your position in the line. (However, there is no good reason for divorced parents to stand next to each other in the line-up, unless they both express a desire to do so.)

In the Jewish tradition, the father's part in the receiving line has always been optional anyway. He can, therefore, gracefully exclude himself without causing a stir. Because of the Jewish tradition of the bride and groom spending time alone together directly after the service, reception lines are often omitted entirely.

Photographs are not part of the wedding ceremony. There is no right or wrong way to set up the shots, except that they should reflect the happy memories that the bridal couple wish to remember. If the bride or groom would like a picture with his or her natural parents on either side of her or him, etiquette suggests this is appropriate. Such a photograph is not an illusionary statement that the parents are still a couple, but it is a memento that reflects the love each parent still holds for the child. It is also appropriate that the stepparents be included in some of the photographs, as well. It is wise and considerate to discuss this ahead of time with your child if you want a specific group shot.

As for the grandparents, it is not unusual today for there to be many sets. Sometimes the stepgrandparents have played a larger role in the children's lives than the natural grandparents. In any case, all these very important people should be included in the festivities. In the Christian wedding, grandparents have no official part. However, they should be treated as special guests. In the Jewish ceremony, they have traditionally been a part of the procession. Even when there are several sets of grandparents, they can all be included. However, it is better to do away with the tradition than to include only some grandparents, causing others to feel left out.

At the reception, grandparents can be seated at their children's (the parents') tables, or, when there are many involved, a separate grandparents' table can be set up especially for them. The wisdom of age often brings an ability and desire to share the joys of the grandchildren with the other grandparents.

As for the rehearsal dinner, it is proper etiquette for the immediate family to be included.

If, for some reason, the bride or groom doesn't want a parent to attend the wedding, then ultimately that parent should respect the wishes of the child. However, it is also important that the parent to be excluded have an opportunity to discuss these issues with the child before automatic exclusion. The parent, by exclusion, may be missing an event that is extremely important to his or her own emotional needs and satisfactions. Should the parent ultimately be excluded from the ceremonies, he or she should be left with the consolation that he or she did everything possible to create situational peace and had an opportunity to make his or her own wishes known. (A note to the bride and groom: Think long and hard before excluding a parent from your wedding. You may long regret the decision, whatever your reasons.)

One last word on weddings. There will probably be times when a perfect solution cannot be found. However, if the focus of the occasion can be kept on the celebration of the marriage and the joy of the bride and groom, situational peace will come much more easily.

It is natural for children to want to share their accomplishments with parents and stepparents. This means that you will sometimes be attending school functions, recitals, and sports events that your children's other parent and/or stepparent are also attending. This does not mean that you have to sit together or socialize. It only requires that you behave civilly and postpone any negative feelings you may have until a more appropriate time.

When children have recitals or special school or sports events, it is not uncommon, but it is certainly unfair, for a parent to tell the children, "If you're inviting your mother [or father], then I'm not going." If your former spouse puts your children in this position, try to be as neutral as possible when discussing it with your children. Be clear that you are very interested in their activities, and would very much like to attend whatever events to which you are invited. Assure them that you do not blame them for wanting to share their accomplishments with the other parent, as well as with yourself, and if that means that occasionally you'll have to miss a program or a recital, perhaps there are other ways they can share those events with you. If they have paintings in a school art show, maybe they could bring them home and share them with you after the show is over. If they are in a recital, perhaps they could perform their routine for you "in a private rehearsal." It is not a good idea, however, to agree to miss every program. A willingness to do this would demonstrate to them that the other parent's manipulative behavior is a successful maneuver, and they may also interpret your consistent absence as a lack of interest

115

on your part, rather than an attempt to help them avoid loyalty issues.

Most summer camps where the children sleep over have parental visiting days. Especially for young children, and children of divorce, these visiting days are very important, because they reassure the kids that they haven't been abandoned. These camps are often located at least several hours from where the children live, and can present another situation in which divorced parents are thrown together to share their child's world.

This was the case for Joe and Susan (from Chapter 3). Their daughter, Bev, invited them both for parents' visiting day. Joe offered to drive Susan up to the camp, and Susan accepted. "I went up with him. I considered alternatives. Drive up separately in my own car. But we would have to meet there anyway, and do things with the children together anyway. So, I thought, what's the point? I'll drive up with him. I can handle the situation with him."

Having the confidence that you can create situational peace for yourself helps put you in control of your own emotions. Susan's confidence was challenged, and she managed beautifully. "On the way up, he was berating me in the car. I was doing everything wrong, and I was the lousiest mother in the world. I mean, the whole thing. And, I looked at him, and I pushed the seat back, I put it in recline, and I went to sleep. I'm not kidding. I went to sleep. This is an hour-and-a-half ride, and I slept the whole way. I awoke just before we got there. And on the way back, Joe was so filled with positive things about Bev, he didn't pick on me."

It is important to note here that Joe made no attempt at creating situational peace, yet Susan was able to produce it by not joining in the fight. She says she and Joe have been invited to several of their girls' parties, which were put on by mutual friends. "We were both invited to them. Two of them we appeared at together. At the beginning it was a little stilted—you know. I felt somewhat uncomfortable. It was a new situation for me. But then, of course, we've had school events since then. It's fine. You know, when I introduce myself, I say, 'I'm Susan, and this is Bev's father, Joe.' Let them figure it out," she says, laughing.

It is important that both parents share in a child's educational life. PTA meetings and school conferences are good avenues. Remember, if your child is having problems in school that are being discussed in a joint meeting between you, your child's other parent, and the teacher, keep your focus on solving the problem, rather than on placing blame for the problem. It will not accomplish anything beneficial to criticize or censure your former spouse, or to remind anyone that "I told you so." The emotions prompting you to do this need to be postponed while you concentrate on the issues at hand.

Graduation exercises present another special occasion where divorced parents need to attend and participate jointly. The importance of this was expressed by 19-year-old Tim, whose parents were divorced seven years ago. It was a bitter divorce, and neither parent had gotten over the hostile feelings each carried for the other. Tim graduated in spring 1990 from a very exclusive prep school in the East, for which his father had paid dearly. Although the cost of the tuition, living expenses, and private tutoring Tim received were actually beyond his father's means (his father had to put more than one payment on a credit card, thus accruing a large interest payment as well), he took on the total financial responsibility for it because he felt his son needed and deserved the benefits the private school could offer. Tim's mother had initially been against sending him to the prep school, feeling it was a ploy to get him away from her, but when Tim's school performance dropped below passing, she reluctantly went along with the school transfer. Tim's extra effort at his new school, his mother's willingness to acquiesce, and his father's financial sacrifice all paid off: Tim successfully completed his senior year.

It was a blow to Tim, however, when his father told him that he didn't want Tim's mother to attend his graduation. "I paid for your school. She didn't pay a dime," his father told him, but Tim fought for the right to have his mother there. "I want her there. She's my mom," Tim told his father, "and that's all the reason I need." Fortunately, Tim's dad relented, and both parents attended his graduation exercises.

"I was a nervous wreck," Tim says. "They hadn't seen each other face to face in four or five years. All I could think of was 'Don't talk to each other. Just don't sit next to each other. I'll be OK.' That part was bad. But they made it through. It was just important to me that they were both there."

One of the least comfortable decisions divorced parents may have to face is the question of whether or not to attend the funeral of a former spouse. Having just lost one parent to death, it may be especially important to your children attending the funeral that you be there for their emotional support. Unless there are special circumstances, such as open hostility toward you from the widow or widower of the deceased, it is proper for you to make an appearance at the funeral home, as well as to attend the service. Choose an inconspicuous seat at the service, however, rather than sitting with the family.

When there is open hostility between you and the new spouse, you may refrain from making a personal appearance; send flowers and a sympathy note instead. (Hopefully, as society becomes more educated in the importance of avoiding these circumstances, it will no longer be an issue.) However, be sure to make yourself particularly accessible to your children during this time. They will need all the reassurance they can possibly get that you are still there for them. If the antagonism between you and your former spouse's widow or widower has been instigated by you, we urge you to at least postpone your animosity so that you can be there for your children.

Birthdays and holidays present a different kind of situation in that they are usually intimate affairs celebrated by the immediate family. Birthdays are especially important to a child because it's the one day of the year that he or she alone is honored. If your family tradition has been to give a large children's party each year, then you and your former spouse are going to have to decide which one of you is going to act as its host. Because birthdays recur, of course, it might make sense to alternate years if you both live in the same area. In any case, your child will probably be thrilled if both parents can be there, even if the nonhost parent only stays for a short while. If it's customary in your family that birthday celebrations are limited to family gatherings, then it is appropriate that you alternate years for the birthday dinner if it is still too uncomfortable for you and your former spouse to share such personal contact. However, some parents do manage even such close encounters on birthdays and holidays.

Holidays are usually assigned in some fashion by the courts at the time of the divorce; and while children would usually prefer to share the holidays with both parents together, most accept that this will no longer be the case. This, however, does not mean that there shouldn't be a shared event. If, for example, it has always been a tradition in your family to attend midnight mass together on Christmas Eve, then you might want to consider keeping this as a part of your holiday celebration.

Because holidays are a time when the custodial parent must often send off the children to spend time with their other parent, it becomes important for the custodial parent to fill in his or her own time as joyously as possible. Holidays can be lonely times, and it is up to you to make sure that yours are not. No one else can do this for you. This is not the time to spend long hours alone dwelling on the past, because this can lead to escalated feelings of anger and hostility. Instead, seek new ways to keep the holidays festive. Even if the children are with you, it's a good idea to "break" some of the old traditions, adding new ones in their place. This is a good time to practice flexibility and change. However, discuss any changes with your children beforehand. They will have set expectations, and there will be certain customs they will want to keep.

Gift-giving holidays and birthdays can be difficult for the less financially well-off parent if there's a large discrepancy between the two incomes of the parents. If you are the parent with lesser means, it is up to you to be tolerant of any expensive gifts your former spouse may give to your children. Rather than looking at these presents as a competitive edge that your former spouse has over you (focusing on yourself), instead look at them as advantages that your children would not otherwise have (focus on your children). Nice things, in and of themselves, will not damage your children, and if their love can actually be bought by a few gifts, then there's a lot more wrong going on in the parenting of these children than the giving of a few material possessions.

If you are the parent spending the holidays without the children, assure them sincerely that you will not be lonely. Don't use your "aloneness" to diminish the good time your children deserve with their other parent. Even older children worry incessantly about a parent spending the holidays without them, and it is not unusual for them to perceive themselves as abandoning you. They should not be burdened with the responsibility of your good time. Spending the holidays alone is a decision made by choice. Even if you have no accessible relatives or friends with whom you can share these times, there are many singles groups or charities that would happily welcome you as a volunteer to help make someone else's celebration more joyous. Again, this is a good time to practice flexibility and change.

In summary, the bitter conflict between you and your former spouse does not have to be resolved in order for you to create situational peace. Although working through your resentments can be a healthy experience, you need not be "over the divorce" for you to share your child's special occasions with his or her other parent. The more skilled you become at managing change, the more likely you are to achieve situational peace.

Moreover, change does not have to feel good for you to manage it. It is OK to feel uncomfortable for short periods of time. The clue to achieving situational peace is to intentionally bar your negative emotions from your consciousness during the event you are attending.

Children need and deserve to have their parents attend the important events of their lives. When you achieve situational peace, you help create an environment in which both you and your children can relax and enjoy the momentous occasions.

Divorced parents should not be excluded from the requirements of good manners. The Golden Rule of Etiquette for divorced parents when planning a special occasion for their child is to *include the other parent*. The focus of the celebration should be on the child.

Chapter

6

Facing the Ex-in-Laws

When divorce occurs, it affects not only spouses and children, but also the extended family—grandparents, aunts, uncles, brothers, sisters, and cousins on both sides of the family, as well as long-time family friends. Chances are your relationship with your former spouse's relatives will change with divorce, and you may find yourself suddenly snubbed, ignored, or even verbally attacked by people you once considered "family." This can be very hurtful, particularly at a time when you may need all the support you can get. It can be difficult under these circumstances to refrain from fighting back, and especially so if you partially blame any of these people for your break-up in the first place. However, it is important that you make every effort to behave in a civil and polite manner toward your former spouse's family network, because, although they are no longer a part of your family, *they are still just as important a part of your children's family as they were before the divorce.*

After the divorce, there may well be a time period when you have little or no contact with your former spouse's family. Even though you will probably see your children's other parent on a fairly regular basis during visitation exchanges, school-related matters, and so on (unless you are geographically separated), a long time may pass before you come face to face with his or her family members. However, eventually you are bound to be thrown together. How you feel about this encounter will depend on many factors, including how you view your present relationship with them, your views on marriage and divorce, your feelings about your own marriage and divorce, and your degree of self-esteem.

If you feel guilty about your divorce, chances are you do not look forward to facing your former in-laws. If you are taking full blame for the dissolution, sort through your reasons for your need to accept fault. Even though you may have instigated the separation, that does not mean that you have committed a wicked act. Taking a wholesome responsibility for your actions is one thing, but carrying around a load of guilt can be unhealthy and unproductive.

Both Christians and Jews view marriage as a religious institution and families as divinely inaugurated structures. Roman Catholics go so far as to regard marriage as a sacrament (instituted or recognized by Christ), and Jews consider it a divine commandment. It is not surprising then that, for those raised in a religious environment, to "break up" the family through divorce may seem worthy of serious guilt. After all, "guilt" is a learned form of penance for religious sin.

If you are suffering anxiety over this, you might want to consider how dramatically the family structure has changed in the last hundred years. (*Note*: Although these changes may have begun in the United States, comparable transitions are found in other Western industrial societies.)

During the first third of this century, most U.S. families were traditional extended families (that is, multigenerational). In this extended family structure, not only parents and children but also grandparents, aunts, uncles, and cousins all formed the family unit. They worked together, played together, learned together, and worshiped together. This was the composition of the "normal" family.

As the economy changed and the work force became more mobile, however, it was no longer financially advantageous for the extended family to exist in that form, and the nuclear family (mother, father, children) became the norm. This type of family flourished in the 1950s in America. The father's role was to be the breadwinner. He was to go out into the world and become financially successful. The mother was to be the homemaker, the caretaker of both the father and the children, and the husband's supportive companion. The family image became very child centered and success oriented.

Then, in the 1960s, there was a definitive rebellion against the family "portrait" of the era. Women no longer wanted to be shackled to their Frigidaires. Men sought self-fulfilment rather than material success. Reliable birth control and modern household inventions freed women to work for wages outside of the home, and that added money freed their husbands to take less responsibility for the family income. This explosion of individualism set the stage for the amazing variety of family structures we have today. In the second half of the 1970s and the 1980s, overt nostalgia for older family values set in, but the family structure itself continued to diversify.

Today we have a number of family units. One form is the one-parent household, which may be headed by widows or widowers, women who have chosen to have children outside of marriage, and separated or divorced people. There are also other family units including, but not limited to, stepfamilies, unmarried couples (cohabitating without legal sanction or benefit of clergy), homosexual households, foster families, grandparent and grandchild families, open marriages, adoptive interracial families, singles households, couples who are childless by choice, and the traditional nuclear family (husband, wife, child). It has also become the rule, rather than the exception, that preschoolers are looked after by caregivers while both parents work full time. This may or may not have future consequences for our society, but it does conflict with the 1950s image of the ideal family. In spite of this expansive list of alternative family forms and arrangements, many people still cling unrealistically to the nuclear form as the "normal" family unit. This refusal (or perhaps time lag) by society to accept itself as it exists today can produce feelings of guilt and failure in people who are divorcing. Once we accept the reality of our changed society, we will more easily accept ourselves within that society. Just as we can no longer *expect* to live and work within an extended family, to hold one job our entire lives, or to retire at age 65, children today can no longer *expect* that all families will have just one set of parents, and we cannot *expect* that all marriages will last until "death do us part." Any of these *might* happen in certain cases, but there are too many exceptions for us to continue considering these exceptions "abnormal."

It is not necessarily the form of the family structure that is crucial to children, but the availability of love and security. Children must be able to count on the love of their parents and other significant adults, and to trust that that love will not be taken away because of a change in the form of the family relationship. If these are the goals that you are working toward, then you deserve to hold your head up proudly when you share your children with your former spouse's family.

EXERCISE

Affirmations

An affirmation is an assertion about yourself. By repeating affirmations over and over again, you can begin to break through your negative beliefs and see yourself in a more positive manner. Your unconscious will believe anything you say, if you repeat it often enough.

1. Make a list of anyone who is likely to attend your child's special event and whose opinion or actions concerning the divorce causes you anxiety.

2. Standing in front of a mirror, look yourself directly in the eye. Using each of the names from the list, repeat the following affirmation several times out loud: "I, (*your name*), am a capable individual, and I can achieve situational peace with (*name of former relative*)."

Practice this exercise every day as you get ready to attend your child's special occasion. As you repeat this affirmation time and again, you will begin to gain confidence in yourself and will develop a healthier way of thinking about the upcoming event.

It is not always the issue of divorce, however, that makes us hesitant to see those former family members and friends. Sometimes it is our physical appearance that makes us shrivel at the thought. If you are a man, it may be your balding head or paunchy belly that you don't want exposed to "those" people, especially if you had a full head of hair and tight abdominals the last time you saw them. And if you are a woman, you are even more apt to be concerned with your looks and appearance.

Beauty has a very powerful place in most cultures, and while each culture defines beauty differently, they all agree on its power. Social interactions teach us the importance of looking good, and women are usually assessed more critically than men on their physical appearance. Attractive people are attributed positive qualities, based on their looks alone. Girl babies are told they are beautiful, while boy babies are more apt to be described as sturdy or strong. Little girls are dressed up and encouraged to inspire praise for their appearance. They learn early that makeup such as lipstick and fingernail polish are intended to make them more attractive, thus instilling the idea that they must not be pretty enough without it. Women often grow up to think they must always look a certain way, and this special look is presently expressed by our mass media.

Our current U.S. culture tells us that the right look is young and thin. By the time a young woman is 20, for example, she's usually considered too old to begin a career in fashion modeling. Most women think there's something wrong with their bodies, because they don't have the same figures as those they see in magazines or on movie screens. Even if a woman is naturally thin, she may feel unattractive because she's not tall enough. A tall, thin woman may be self-conscious because her breasts aren't the "right" size or shape. A tall, thin, round-breasted woman may be obsessed with her thick ankles, and so on *ad infinitum,* and while people of other cultures may admire different physical qualities, they can also become obsessed with attaining their own physical ideals. So it's not surprising that you, too, may be concerned with your physical appearance, how it compares with the last time you saw your former relatives, and how it compares with your former spouse's present significant other.

But our culture's unrealistic standards for eternal youth and "magazine"-style body configurations are only as valid as we accept them to be. Demanding them of ourselves can be damaging. It can lead to fad diets, anorexia, bulimia, and other eating disorders. It can prompt us to make unhealthy decisions about cosmetic surgery. It can lead us to avoid attending our children's special events for fear that one of "those" people might think we've aged (which, of course, we have) or that we're not as thin as we once were.

The first question you should ask yourself if you are bothered about seeing your former relatives because of your appearance is "Am I really dissatisfied with the way I look, or is my present dissatisfaction based on my worries about what my former relatives will think?" If you find your anxiety is based primarily on what your former spouse's family will think of you, then you need to consider why their opinions are so important to you. Why are you still seeking their approval? It may be out of habit; you simply haven't taken the time to redefine your relationship to them. Once you recognize that these people's opinions need no longer concern you, you will feel confident to face them again as the person you have become, rather than as the person they once knew when you were "family." Unless you have a relationship with them that has superseded the divorce (in which case you've probably seen them on a somewhat regular basis), you can feel free of the pressure to compete for their attention or approval.

If, however, *you* actually are dissatisfied with your appearance, regardless of what others think, then you have some work to do. You can either learn to accept your appearance, or you can change it. If you decide you want to change it, make sure you are doing it to please yourself, not others. Once you're sure of this, then you have options, depending on what it is you want to change. If your body size is making you anxious, consider exercise, a change of diet, and/or cosmetic surgery. If you make any of these choices, it is important to note that good judgment dictates healthy moderation and good nutrition. It is also worthy of mention here that while exercise stimulates the release of endorphins, which act to improve the disposition and create a "natural high," starvation diets tend to produce anxiety and feelings of deprivation. Cosmetic surgery is expensive and, as with any surgery, can be risky.

If you decide that you'd like to become more accepting of your body size, then you might want to learn that most women *over*estimate their own body size. They see themselves as heavier than they are, maybe because of the constant comparisons they make between themselves and magazine fashion models. People who are unhappy with their body size are also often obsessed with weight. The sight of an additional two pounds on the scale in the morning can throw them into a depressed mood for the whole day. Most women are afraid of getting fat, and tend to overreact to any weight gain.

If you want to learn to accept your body size the way it is—even if you're larger-boned or thicker-hipped than what the media projects as ideal—then become more flexible in your attitude toward body size. We all come in different sizes and shapes, and you need to accept that if you are going to expand your mental "standard of weights and measures."

EXERCISE

Gaining Flexibility in Body-Size Attitudes

Here is an exercise to loosen up your attitudes toward body size:

1. Make a list of the people you care most about— your best friends, your siblings, your parents, or anyone else whom you respect and admire, leaving some blank space between each name.

2. When you're finished, go back down the list one by one, and write down what you like most about each person.

3. Now read what you've written, and circle each description that refers to the person's body dimensions.

Chances are, there are few circles on your paper. People aren't usually important to us just because they look a certain way. If, however, you find that physical appearance is the most important trait you look for in your friends, then perhaps you will want to change your physical appearance as discussed earlier. Or perhaps you will want to analyze your value system to discover why you rank physical appearance so high.

For those of you who find a few circles on your paper, go through the list again, and this time visualize each person, one by one. Do they all conform to the "perfect" body shape? Probably not, yet that doesn't stop you from liking them "most." If you can accept them with their body imperfections, then it's time to begin working toward accepting yourself as you are.

In addition to becoming more tolerant of your body size, refocus your attention from the parts of your body you dislike, to the parts of your body you find attractive.

EXERCISE

Creating a Positive Body Image

You'll need privacy and a full-length mirror for this exercise. Disrobe down to your underwear.

1. Stand in front of a full-length mirror, and slowly scan your body upward from your feet to your head. Don't stop at any particular area, but try to get an overall sense of what your body looks like.

2. Now, starting over, slowly move your eyes up. When you come to a part of your body you feel is pleasing (such as the graceful high arches of your feet or your well-shaped calves), stop and focus on

this area. Touch it. Admire it. Concentrate on it. Tell yourself that this pleasing part of you is where you want your self-image to begin.

3. Once you feel in touch with that segment of your body, let your eyes wander upward until you come to another pleasing area (perhaps the bend of your knee or the silky skin of your inner thighs). Concentrate on that part of your body as you did in step 2.

Repeat this exercise, giving attention to all the various features that you find pleasing. These are the parts of your body to begin focusing on, rather than on the areas you don't like. As you duplicate this exercise each day or so, you'll begin to see your body in a more positive way.

One more note to remember about your body size as you mentally prepare to meet your former relatives: it might be helpful to realize that, even if *you* are focused on your thickened waist, most people *won't* be. For example, at your child's graduation party, the attention of the guests will probably be on the young graduate, not on your waistline. (Sometimes giving up the illusion of taking center stage has advantages.)

Some people never seem to age. Others do, and quite visibly. If you feel you look a lot older than the last time you saw your former relatives, and this concept bothers you, then you need to make some changes.

Again, these changes can be physical and/or mental. If you choose to make physical changes, they can be short term, such as a hair color change or a makeup makeover, or longer term, as through cosmetic surgery. New technologies and surgery techniques now provide many alternatives for a more youthful look. There are hair transplants, face lifts, collagen injections, and eyelid tucks, just to name a few. However, carefully analyze your motives when you consider any long-term changes, because you should not let one current need, such as confronting your former relatives, trigger a major course of action such as surgery, with its high cost and risk factors. Also, chances are good that your child's family will learn about your surgery anyway. You will not be keeping them "fooled" as to your appearance.

Our perceptions of looking older are often tied to our concepts of aging. If we consider everyone over age 35 to be over the hill, mentally unstimulating, and socially dull, then chances are we will regard gray hair as unattractive, less elasticity in the skin to be unappealing, and lines in the face to be offensive. However, if we have role models we admire who represent many different age groups, then we will probably have a more flexible tolerance for settling bodies and balding heads.

As with body size, women are more apt than men to be criticized or ignored because they look older, and therefore are more likely to be concerned by it. The double standard of physical aging is real. Although many men face a midlife crisis, it is rarely brought on by a receding hairline or the discovery of gray at their temples. Society is somewhat forgiving of the aging of men, but it discourages aging in women.

Cosmetic companies urge women to maintain a youthful appearance. Older actresses often find themselves out of work. Female television anchors get dumped for younger replacements. Society's message is clear: "don't look old." Yet while the message is certainly aimed toward women, men can also suffer from anxiety over the loss of a youthful appearance.

So you may imagine yourself as looking too old to face your former relatives, yet you may hesitate to make changes in your appearance. This is not a contradiction, for many people have inner conflicts over their desire to "look like themselves" and their wish to look pleasing to others. If you are struggling with this issue, you may want to strengthen your own positive feelings about aging before making a decision.

EXERCISE
Visualizing Role Models

Here is a way to approach positive feelings about aging:

1. Make a list of the people throughout history, and from your own experiences, whom you most admire. Take your time, and think about what they've accomplished.
2. Now go back through your list, and visualize the face of each person. Once you get a clear image in your mind, write down the age of the person as you see him or her in your imagination.

Chances are that most of the people you thought of were older than 30. If not, perhaps you might want to broaden your scope on accomplishments you consider worthy of admiration, because the fact is that many people achieve their greatest success after their youth has long since evaporated. Most of us do our finest work, achieve our highest goals, and acquire our greatest wisdom in our later years. These accomplishments are also a part of aging, and our sagging skin and crow's-feet are reflections of our progress.

A final note on your appearance. A radiant smile transcends age. Sparkling eyes reflect inner vitality and strength. A sense of humor draws admiration and elicits joy. If you can radiate confidence, charm, and warmth, you'll leave them speechless.

Although society places more pressure on women than men to look good, the opposite is true when it comes to financial success. Women are supposed to "have" financial success, but men are supposed to "produce" it (or, in the case of inherited wealth, they're supposed to increase it). That is not to diminish the role of women today in the workplace, but it is to say that by society's standards a woman can be considered successful if she marries well and does her share of volunteer work. However, both men and women are rated by their economic standing in the community, regardless of where the money comes from. This financial measure of personal worth can pressure people to do something or marry someone to guarantee them the same status they enjoyed in their previous marriage. Loss of this economic status can become a stumbling block to someone about to face his or her former "family."

One maneuver is to create a deceptive image for the day. Someone may hire a limousine, rent expensive jewelry, inflate his or her job titles, brag about yachts and exotic travel, and pretend to be someone richer. Of course, the down side of this social hypocrisy is that it can make the imposter feel shallow and phony, and can lead to even worse embarrassment if he or she is found out.

Only people who buy into the theory that "the value of a person is directly proportional to the size of his or her bank account" feel the undue pressure of not measuring up financially. Once you are satisfied with *yourself*, you will no longer feel competitive with your former spouse, because reaching the goals *you* value will solidify your self-esteem.

Self-esteem comes from within. When you try to build your self-esteem from external sources (income, appearances), you are setting yourself up for a letdown. When you turn your self-worth over to others to define, you give up your right to set your own goals.

If you have let material possessions become the sole basis for your self-acceptance, work on accepting yourself for who you are, rather than for what you can buy. True self-esteem is based on the unconditional conviction that you are lovable, deserving, and virtuous. When you put conditions on this worthiness, you put your self-acceptance on very shaky ground.

Many people see themselves only through the eyes or the values of others. If they do something that makes someone react in a certain fashion, this reaction is deposited into their "self-esteem bank." They only feel valuable as human beings when someone else verifies their value. They are people who only feel good about themselves when others are giving them approval. Once the approval diminishes, so does their self-esteem.

Take, for instance, the following two artists. Jena studies her craft with a boundless amount of energy. She never seems to stop sketching and works constantly to improve her technique. After years of preparation, Jena finally lands her first show in a small gallery in New England. The turnout is disappointing. The reviews are nonexistent. The revenue is minimal. Yet *she* believes in her work. She is disappointed, but her self-esteem remains intact. Jena continues to pursue her love of painting.

The second artist, Max, has never bothered to study art, but does have a certain natural flair. When a high-powered gallery owner in New York "discovers" his work, she gives Max a show, making him an instant success. His work is suddenly in demand. He paints from morning until night, cranking out one piece after another. For an entire year he's hot, and his self-esteem is soaring. However, as with most shooting stars, his ride is short-lived. By the next year the gallery owner has discovered a new "starlet," and Max's work is put on the back burner. His self-esteem is all but extinguished, and he puts away his brushes for good.

Jena's self-esteem is driven by internal values. She believes in her work and in herself whether the rest of the world applauds her efforts or not. Max's self-esteem is measured by external events. He feels good about himself and his art only when others approve. Once the approval is gone, so is his belief in himself.

That is one of the dangers of basing your self-esteem on what you produce rather than on who you are. External conditions change. Real estate markets dry up, leaving developers jobless. Recessions hit, leaving consumers without the income to support fine arts. Corporations merge, eliminating certain positions. Technologies change, putting long-established companies out of business. A change in external conditions, however, does not mean that your value *as a person* is heightened or diminished. You don't deserve to lose your self-esteem because outside circumstances beyond your control are in constant transition.

No one else can make you feel bad about yourself without your permission. However, they may try. Fortunately, you can learn skills to combat their efforts.

The first thing you can do when someone attempts to undermine your self-esteem is to consider the source. Perhaps some people at your child's event, out of feelings of jealousy, intimidation, and so on, really would like to see your self-image diminished. There will be nothing you can do to stop them from trying, but you can show one-up-manship by behaving civilly and politely through it all. Remember, it is very disheartening to people when their nasty attacks are met with graciousness and dignity.

Another strategy you can use to diminish the effect of someone else's negative remarks is to avoid taking the other person's comments personally. Often people lash out at others because they themselves face frustrations, and their anger may actually have very little to do with you. And even if hurtful remarks *are* directed toward you, they have only the validity you give them.

If someone at the affair becomes loud and abusive (which is very unlikely), you can simply get away from that person. Nothing in the rules of etiquette requires you to stand there and be ridiculed. Simply say, "Please excuse me, but I don't wish to speak about it here." Then, glancing behind you, take two steps back, turn, and walk away.

You can now comfortably seek out anyone else with whom you would like to speak. Again, if you can retain your class and decorum, you will enjoy the respect of all those worthy of it.

If you feel this would be letting your attacker get away with something, reconsider the dynamics of the situation. Someone has created a disturbance, and it is up to you to handle the conflict as swiftly and graciously as possible. You are not in combat with someone who needs defeating. You are in a situation that needs defusing as soon as possible. Don't concentrate on causing the other person to look bad (that's already been accomplished by his or her actions), and don't worry about defending yourself. The important thing is to restore peace and harmony to the festivities. Once you have accomplished that, you have won the skirmish.

If a challenging remark is made by someone whom you think may simply be testing the waters for a possible rekindling of your relationship, you might treat it with humor. Suppose your former spouse's old roommate approaches you with a dig about your reduced financial circumstances: "Well, it looks like Cinderella's not doing so well without her Prince Charming." You might respond with something like "Ouch . . . that hurt. Don't step on my glass slipper like that."

Moreover, don't jump to the conclusion, because someone makes a negative remark, that the comment was directed at you. For example, if you hear your former sister-in-law talking about the unattractiveness of bald men, don't assume she's talking about you because you're bald. If your former mother-in-law cuts in front of you in the buffet line, don't assume it's because she wants to push you out of the way. If your former brother-in-law, in introducing you, gets your new married name wrong, or attributes a lower job title to you than you really enjoy, or in some other way reduces your status, don't assume it's done to diminish you.

Your former sister-in-law may simply be expressing her preference for men with thick locks. She may have just started dating a heavily mopped man, or she may be afraid that her own husband is losing his hair. Your former mother-in-law may have cut in front of you simply because she was hungry. Your brother-in-law may suffer from a short memory, or he, himself, might be nervous talking with you after your long separation. Never suppose a malicious intent if incompetence, stupidity, or insensitivity are even remote possibilities. In many cases the offending parties are simply speaking or acting for themselves, and their actions have no intentional messages for you.

If you do have to suffer hurtful comments, remember the affirmation exercise earlier in this chapter and repeat it to yourself over and over again, because you *are* a capable individual, and you *can* achieve situational peace with these people. If you don't get their respect, consider the fact that those who criticize others are often projecting their own insecurities and dissatisfaction with themselves. Remember, you can't control other people's behavior, but you can control your own self-image.

Another strategy for preparing yourself to face a resentful former relative, or any disagreeable person, is to develop empathy for their feelings. Try putting yourself in "their shoes," and see if you can relate to how they might be feeling. That does not mean you have to agree with the way they think, but it does suggest that you consider the circumstances behind their behavior.

Julie's divorced parents and stepparents were all invited to her wedding. Julie's stepmother, Iris, was nervous about attending the wedding, because Julie's natural mother would be there. To begin with, although Julie had once been very close to Iris, and had even lived with her and Julie's father at one time, their relationship had suffered over the past several years, and now Iris wasn't sure how she fit into Julie's life. Secondly, Julie's family had always considered her natural mother to be a beautiful woman, and this was also somewhat disconcerting to Iris. As the day of the wedding approached, she confided her concerns to her sister, Martha.

Before the service, Martha got on the wedding video-tape microphone and made a speech about Iris, referring to her as Julie's "mother" and glorifying her beauty and mothering skills. At first, Julie's natural mother was taken aback, but as she sat there listening, she tried to put herself in Martha's place. To begin with, it was apparent that Martha loved her sister dearly and wanted to defend and reassure her. Because Julie's mother loved her own sister deeply, she could identify with Martha's feelings. The speech also clearly reflected Iris's apparent concerns about her relationship with Julie—more feelings Julie's mother could relate to. As Martha was extolling Iris's merits, Julie's mother tried to share Martha's frame of reference, and by empathizing with her was able to disengage any need she may have otherwise felt to justify her own position as Julie's mother.

No matter what your feelings are on coming face to face with your former spouse's relatives, keep your conversations with them unemotional during your child's special affair. However trivial this chit-chat may seem, it will be productive if it helps keep everything on an even keel. Keep your comments neutral and focused on the event or on your child. Your purpose or role of the day is to support your child and share in her or his joy, not to engage in verbal combat. If negative emotions gurgle up, swallow them. It won't hurt you to postpone them until after the affair. If positive feelings for a particular guest are renewed, set a future date for the two of you to talk. Again, this is not a good place to discuss emotional issues, even if they center around re-established affections. The reason for this is that what may start out as a rekindling of old friendships could burst into flames of anger if the wrong thing is said, or if the right thing is said in the wrong way. Feelings will be sensitive, and this is not the place to test their resilience.

In summary, remember that what you focus your attention on grows in importance. Keep your thoughts positive and centered on your child and on the occasion. When you become preoccupied by feelings of inadequacy, you are doing yourself and your child an injustice to his or her special event.

As family structures become more diverse, it becomes even more important to sustain the sources of love and security that your children need and deserve. One strategy for accomplishing this is to increase your own self-esteem. Don't let yourself get caught up in guilt or self-loathing.

As you prepare to face your former family and friends, work on positive changes to make the occasion less anxiety-filled for you. If you are unhappy about your physical appearance, change those things you have control over, and learn to accept those you don't. Try not to let your financial status determine your self-acceptance.

Learn how to protect your self-esteem, and how to be gracious under pressure. Practice affirmations that reinforce your dignity. Try to empathize with former relatives who see things differently. Above all, learn to love yourself in spite of imperfections.

▼

Chapter

7

Including Your Ex's New Spouse

The following letter was written by a mother to her ex-husband's wife. The wife was the "other woman" before the divorce and is now her children's stepmother.

Dear Julia,

I thought it was time I wrote to thank you for being there for Wendy and Tommy. I know it hasn't always been easy for you, and that I haven't always been as cooperative or appreciative as I might have been.

Being a stepparent must sometimes feel like the most thankless job in the world. I know, from being a mother myself, that there are a million little jobs that need attending to every day; preparing meals the kids don't want to eat, washing the clothes they don't want to wear, giving reminders they don't want to hear, or encouraging the homework they hate. I know getting up in the middle of the night to attend to a sick or scared child can be exhausting. Trips to the dentist, cheerleading practice, and Boy Scouts can all make one feel more like a taxi driver than a parent.

I also know how the kids take all this for granted. While it's hard enough for parents to knock themselves out day after day and year after year without hearing any particular sign of appreciation, it must be especially tough on a stepparent.

I'm sure you must know that Wendy and Tommy love you very much. I don't know if they think to say "thank you" for all that you do for them. Probably not, because they consider you as one of their parents, and as such, they expect these things from you.

I wanted you to know how much I appreciate your interest and concern for the kids. While I miss them terribly when they're with you, I never worry that they're not being cared for and loved. Thank you for being the stepparent that you are.

With Appreciation,

L

This mother's attitude toward her children's stepmother was motivated, not by a desire to become friends with her, but by a concern for her children's welfare. She understood that children want and need both their natural parents in their lives, and that this often means that stepparents may also become important people in their children's lives. She realized that stepparents are not a threat to the love that children have for their natural parents. They are considered by children to be additions to, rather than as replacements for, their mothers and fathers.

A child's love for a parent doesn't evaporate because of the addition of a counterpart or parallel stepparent (mother, stepmother; father, stepfather) to a child's life, yet many parents fear this might happen. They may feel threatened, afraid that a stepparent will replace them. Perhaps they worry if their children call their stepfather "Dad," or fear their kids will be enchanted by their stepmother's youthful style. Noncustodial parents may worry that the stepparent—a person they may not even know, or worse yet, may dislike—will be spending more time with their children than they do themselves. The day-to-day care of the children may very well be placed in the hands of the stepmother, and the noncustodial mother may worry that the stepmother and her values will have the greatest influence over her children.

Some noncustodial parents become so threatened by the addition of a stepparent to their children's lives that they withdraw both physically and/or emotionally, convinced that they're going to be replaced by the "interlopers." Ironically, this very withdrawal by the parents can cause their children to turn to the stepparents for love and care not being given by the natural mother or father. So the natural parent's prophecy becomes a reality. A child's need for continuity in his or her life becomes stronger when there is a major change such as the addition of a stepparent to the family. A natural parent's withdrawal at this stage can be especially hurtful and confusing.

Parents who stay involved with their children do not have to worry about losing a child's love to a stepparent. First, as mentioned earlier, *children consider stepparents to be* additional *people in their lives, not replacements for their natural parents.* This cannot be stressed enough. As long as the parent remains involved with the child, the child will not lose his or her attachment to the parent (and may not, even if the parent does not remain involved). Secondly, often stepparents don't *want* to be replacements for their stepchildren's parents. In fact, stepparents sometimes don't even like their stepchildren, and more often don't want any more responsibility for them than the situation requires. Just as children love their natural parents unconditionally, so also natural parents (and most adoptive parents, especially when the child was adopted as an infant) are usually the only ones who love their children unconditionally. Usually no one loves your children as much as you do, except for their other parent.

A stepparent's desire to take over as sole mother or father is usually overestimated. To begin with, no matter how much people protest this notion, a certain pride is inherent in creating a child who has your genes. The child represents to the parent a little piece of his or her own immortality. A stepparent, of course, does not feel this connection. This heredity link is not necessary for unconditional love to exist, but it does mean that a stepparent cannot develop that particular bond.

Secondly, most stepparents don't come into a child's life until after at least part of the child's personality has been formed. Although parents may dislike certain personality traits in their own children, even more often personality conflicts exist between children and their stepparents. These conflicts can be exacerbated when the child also has habits that are unattractive to the stepparent.

Many stepparents, like parents, come into the job with no parenting skills or experience, and no concept of what it means to coparent a child. Some stepparents have the unrealistic idea that the child is going to adore them immediately, love them profusely, and thank them consistently for their sacrifices. As stepparents start to catch on to the reality of the situation, and begin to feel the first inklings of rejection (which occur even in the best of circumstances), they may feel impatience and anger. This can lead to more frustration for the child and hostility toward the stepparent.

"Terrific," you may be thinking. "I don't want my children exposed to the bastard [or hussy]. The less they have to do with him [or her], the better off they'll be." Even if your feelings aren't quite that negative, you may still relish every denunciation of the stepparent you hear from your children. "What's wrong with that?" you may ask. "Why do I want to promote a relationship between my children and someone I hate . . . or *would* hate if I knew him [or her]?"

The reason you will want to promote a positive relationship between your children and your stepparent counterpart is because, whether you like it or not, that person is going to be significant in your children's lives. *It will be healthier and nicer for your children if they can get along with and feel comfortable with that stepparent.* It will even be more gratifying for them if they can develop, over time, a loving relationship with this person. It is appropriate for you to do everything you can to promote a positive relationship between your children and their stepparent. Also, your children need your permission to do so.

The first and most important thing you can do is to assure your children that they can love both you and their stepmother or stepfather, and that to love their stepparent is not being disloyal to you. Words alone will probably not convince them of this, because often children feel that loving the new mate of one parent *is* being unfaithful to the other parent. They think that in order to love a stepmother or stepfather, they must give up the love they have for their natural mother or father—which they are not willing to do. So instead they get angry at the stepparent and refuse to open themselves up to a relationship with him or her. This can strain the relationship between the children and their other parent, which can be damaging and hurtful to the children.

Also, when children begin to develop affection for their stepparent, they may suffer from feelings of disloyalty. Especially if the stepparent's counterpart natural parent shows a dislike for the stepparent, the children may develop feelings of guilt and unfaithfulness. And if the children overhear their parents arguing about a significant other, they will have bad feelings about this person. However, a parent's dislike for a parallel stepparent doesn't have to be overt to be picked up by the children. Because they tend to believe loving a natural parent and a parallel stepparent is inherently disloyal, children will be overly sensitive to any signs of conflict between the two. So you should help your children feel they can openly express their emotions about their stepparent without any judgmental repercussions from you. You can encourage them to talk about experiences they have with their stepparent, and you can show pleasure when these events are positive. With enough reassurances and consistent support from you, your children can gradually learn to feel more comfortable about establishing a relationship with their stepparent. Also, you have some responsibility to do so for the sake of the child's other parent.

You do not have to like your children's stepparent to appreciate the importance of a positive relationship between him or her and your children. Imagine that you are the child who has been through the trauma of your parents' break-up. You already feel torn loyalties between your mother and your father. No matter which parent you're with, you miss the other, and question whether he or she is getting along OK without you. You try your best to "keep things even."

Then, what may seem like suddenly, this new person comes into your mother's or father's life. You ask if your niche in your parent's heart will be taken up by this intruder. You know this addition to your other parent's life means you must give up hopes of your parents reuniting. You may have even been told that this interloper is responsible for your parents' divorce. You're afraid any affection you show toward this person will mean disloyalty to your counterpart parent. Now, in spite of all these concerns, fears, and confusion, you learn that you must spend time with this person regardless of how you feel. Under these circumstances, wouldn't you want to be reassured by your parallel parent that it's OK to feel comfortable with your other parent's new significant other? Wouldn't it make your life seem more secure and less threatening?

You can take steps to help alleviate the torn loyalties your children may be feeling and also to help them adjust to the presence of the new stepparent in their lives. To begin with, your tone of voice implies a lot when you discuss the stepparent. Keep your voice even and your expression positive, focusing on the stepparent as a new friend in your children's lives. He or she is a friend on whom they may need to count for meal preparation, laundry, medical emergencies, and nursing through childhood illnesses, comforting through homesickness or hurt feelings, and financial help. (Stepparents can have a large influence on a noncustodial parent as to whether he or she keeps up child support payments, or on a custodial parent as to where the child support payments are spent. They also usually make a financial investment of their own in your children, through gifts and money for "extras.") Your children benefit when their relationship with a stepparent is positive and healthy.

Avoid making negative comments or giving false impressions about the stepparent. If it has been put into your children's head about the stepfather that "he took Mommy away from you," this error should be addressed directly. Tell your children that Mommy did not belong to you, because people are not possessions. Assure them that both their mother and stepfather made the decision to get together, and that no one "takes" another person away from a relationship in which they are completely happy.

Do not subtly suggest that the stepparent is a bad person. One father told his 3- and 5-year-olds who were on their way to meet their mother's fiancé that if he ever spanked them, to tell Daddy immediately and he would call the police and have him put in jail. Of course, this suggested to the children that their future stepfather *would* try to spank them, and that he must be a bad person if was going to go to *jail*. The children were both in their late teens before they were able to completely trust their stepfather, and this lack of trust was complicated by the fact that they were both strongly drawn to him. During their growing-up years, they didn't remember what their own father had told them, and so had no idea why they were afraid of their stepfather. However, his words when they were very young caused them real emotional conflicts that were hurtful and unnecessary.

The next issue that stepparents face is the role of disciplinarian. The last thing children usually hope for is another adult in their lives with the authority to discipline them. Chances are that their first reaction to their stepparent's attempt to exercise some form of constraint over them will be to shout, "*You* can't tell me what to do!" It is up to you to assure them that a stepparent *can* expect to set guidelines for their behavior. With small children, discipline can be for their own safety. Children who are told they don't have to do what they're told will not differentiate between not having to eat their spinach and not touching the electric cords. Some authority has to exist for their own physical good.

Children need to grow up knowing where our culture draws the line on acceptable behavior. Without some sense of rules and regulations in both homes, children of divorced parents will get a lopsided view of society's expectations. To think that only the natural parent will have authority over your children in their other home is un-realistic and does not help develop your children's sense of order.

It can be difficult to support your children's step-parent's right to set rules and guidelines when they are substantially different from your own. It can also present a dilemma for your children. For example, suppose you believe that young women should be able to wear make-up if they want to, but your daughter's father and step-mother are opposed to it. Now, we are not talking about an issue here of right and wrong, but one of alternative lifestyles. Your daughter may be trying to work out the kind of value to put on what you say, as opposed to what her stepmother says. It can be difficult for young people to accept, without feeling disloyal, that two different life-styles can both be acceptable. This situation can present a good time for you to talk with her about acceptable alter-natives within any society.

One particularly interesting scenario was related by a well-adjusted mother in this situation. Her son, Chris-topher, is 13. She is white, highly educated, very liberal, socially active, and a political Democrat. Christopher's father is black, Episcopalian, a die-hard Republican, also well educated, and conservative. Christopher's mother is far more lenient with him than his father is, but each sup-ports the other's right to set guidelines in his or her own home. Christopher's mother says, "If Christopher ever showed up at his father's home with one of those smoke-stack hair-dos, or a ghetto blaster on his shoulder, his father would die!" (*She laughs.*) "Christopher's adolescence is go-ing to be funny. He won't know what to rebel against or what to reject. He won't know which end is up, so he'll probably give it up and just be nice."

We are all medleys of our experiences, and you can no more stop children from modeling themselves after

a stepparent than you can stop them from modeling themselves after an aunt, a teacher, or a peer. Young people
sometimes admire traits in stepparents that they want to
emulate. Occasionally this happens without the child even
being consciously aware of it. Other times they try on man-
nerisms, ambitions, or values as though they were trying
out a new hair style. They copy it, wear it for a while, see
if it feels comfortable on them, and then either keep it
or reject it, depending on how it suits them personally.
It's healthy for children to be exposed to different ways
of thinking and acting. When a parent tries to dissuade
this kind of experimentation, it usually leads to rebellion
from the child, either at the time or down the road. If you
try too hard to discourage your children from modeling
themselves after a stepparent, you will probably end up
pushing them to do exactly that.

If your child decides to emulate a stepparent, don't
assume he or she's being encouraged to do so. Parents
sometimes feel a need to protect their young from what
they see as competitive influences from a stepparent, often
justifying their position by labeling the stepparent as
"wrong," only to realize years later that the stepparent was
only trying to fulfill his or her responsibility in providing
the child with a happy, healthy environment.

Children sometimes tell the counterpart parent that
they "hate" their stepparent. This does *not* necessarily
mean that they do. They may be testing your reaction, trying to discern if you *want* them to hate their stepparent.
Again, it can be a loyalty issue. A child may be saying, "Can
I love both a mom and a stepmom, or must I hate one
if I love the other?" Assure your children that they don't
have to pick one over the other. "I hate my stepmother
[or stepfather]," may simply be a way of asking your permission *not* to hate him or her. Give it to them.

It is important to realize the differences between the
parent–child relationship and the stepparent–stepchild

relationship. To begin with, they stem from different beginnings. Most parents today have children because they choose to. It is a conscious decision. Not so for the stepparent—seldom does a person make a conscious choice to become a stepparent. Instead, a person chooses to marry another person, *in spite of the fact that there may be children involved.* Considering the circumstances, it's surprising that most stepparents are willing, and often eager (although perhaps frightened), to take on responsibilities in helping to raise someone else's child.

Most parents experience a natural bonding with their children that takes place from the beginning of the child's life. A child's strongest sense of him- or herself is based on his relationship with his parents, and this connection runs deep. Stepparents, of course, do not usually have this early bonding with these children as infants, or even as toddlers, so that by the time the stepparent arrives on the scene, the child's personality traits and habits have been at least partially formed. There is no guarantee that the stepparent and stepchild will have compatible personalities, and while this is also occasionally true in parent–child relationships, they at least have the early bonding process, which can often override a personality clash.

It is hard for any parent to take rejection from his or her children, but a parent who has already been rejected by a spouse may be particularly sensitive to feeling renounced or abandoned. Therefore divorced parents may be more susceptible to feelings of displacement when their children reject them. Yet a child's growing up involves establishing his or her own identity, and part of this process entails abandonment of some of the parents' attitudes and beliefs. It is not unusual for divorced parents who feel this withdrawal by their child to mistakenly think that they are being replaced by a stepparent.

What the natural parent often fails to realize is that even stepparents who have good relationships with their stepchildren endure continual rejection from them—and most stepparents are not as well equipped to handle it as natural parents are. When a stepparent is rejected by a stepchild, it's a different feeling from what a parent feels when he or she is brushed off by his or her natural child. When your child rejects you, you may feel hurt, but deep down you suspect that you are still loved. This is probably due in part to the early bonding between you and your child.

Not so with a stepparent. Each and every rejection is a reminder he or she is not the child's *real* parent. Stepparents seem to set up unrealistic expectations of the love and appreciation they'll receive from their stepchildren, and although they may eventually get appreciation, it's only after years of thankless effort on their part. And then, if and when it does come, the appreciation is in the form of love for the stepparent as an additional individual in their lives, rather than as love for a parent replacement.

Many stepparents have to deal with very difficult, unhappy children who might otherwise be more accepting of them if it weren't that a parent was sabotaging the relationship. Dotie was initially thrilled when her 11-year-old stepdaughter decided to move in with her, her son, and her husband. "I thought it was going to be different," she says, "but I thought it was going to be wonderful. I thought it would be a breeze," she laughs. "Oh yes, I did, because I think Carrie [her stepdaughter] had had a hard time. I'd listened to her father's end of the phone conversations with her while she was living with her mother, and he'd say, 'Don't cry. You'll be here soon.' My understanding was that she felt wretched being separated from her daddy; that she couldn't wait to come and live with him. And when I met her, she just glommed on, you know, like a little sucker, right up against my side. She loved my son. Oh, god. It was *Good Housekeeping* come true. It was. The perfect suburban family: two children, a dog, a house, a yard, beach trips," she laughs.

Dotie says that the "ideal household" lasted about a year. During that year Carrie kept up contact with her mother through letter writing and telephone calls, and she also spent the summer with her. Throughout the whole year, Carrie's mother consistently displayed distress and grief over her child's "abandonment" of her, and she kept up an emotional warfare over the situation. Finally Carrie could no longer handle her feelings of disloyalty. "I don't know," Dotie says, "Carrie just, it seems to us, she simply suddenly stopped talking to us, and was nasty and unpleasant and sullen. We were just thrown for a loop. We used to just sit there and stare at each other, asking ourselves, 'What happened? What'd we do?' I don't think we'll ever understand what happened."

Carrie continued to live with her stepmother and father until she graduated from high school. Dotie explains, "I enjoyed having a daughter, step or otherwise. When Carrie was feeling good about things, she was very funny. She has a wonderful sense of humor when she feels like it. She can be full of energy, and she likes to get up and go and do things. So it was fun. We'd go bowling. We'd go on picnics. She was *great* with my son. The three of us would conspire to spray her father with shaving cream or surprise him with a barbeque dinner or the four of us would go to the beach, *when* she was happy. On those occasions when she was happy, she was wonderful fun. It was nice to talk to another female in the household. It was fun to giggle and cavort and shop for clothes. Do girlish things. I really enjoyed it very much."

Carrie couldn't manage the good feelings she had about her stepmother because her mother refused to give her permission to feel good about Dotie, and encouraged her to feel guilty about the positive feelings she had. The mental conflict this created finally wore on Carrie to the point where she felt angry, and felt a need to direct this anger toward someone. So Dotie received a letter from Carrie, who was by then away at college. In it Carrie told her stepmother that she thought Dotie was without emotion, tough, unfeeling, and uncaring. Dotie says, "I wanted to assure Carrie that it's not that I'm unfeeling. After all those years of *my* weeping and crying, I am very much convinced I had a lot of feeling." It wasn't Dotie's lack of caring, but Carrie's inability to accept it, that made Carrie strike out at her stepmother.

Whether your children are comfortable with their stepparents or not, they will probably be spending a significant amount of time with them. It is no positive reflection on you if your children are unable or unwilling to establish a healthy relationship with their stepparent. And it may be damaging to them if they can't overcome their feelings of disloyalty toward you when dealing with him or her.

It is important for you to focus on the stepparent as a significant person in your children's lives, rather than as an ally of your former spouse, or as your adversary. Where your children are concerned, everyone should be acting as allies. This is easier when you recognize that the relationship between your former spouse and his or her significant other has no longer anything to do with you, but the announcement of the upcoming marriage of a former spouse can sometimes ignite old feelings you thought were behind you.

Thirty-five-year-old Crystal dreaded her former husband's forthcoming nuptials. "The most difficult time for me, actually, was when he remarried," she says. "Perhaps because I was not going to remarry. I made that decision, and so I just assumed that I would have this awful day when he did. I just assigned a lot of power to this whole situation. So I got ahold of some girlfriends and made plans for the day of his wedding. I bought a bottle of wine and tried to create this real comfort zone. As the day went on, I thought, 'He's getting married right now, and all the kids are there,' and I realized I didn't really care. I had assumed I was going to have this sense of loss, this kind of amputation, but it just never happened. When I had that experience, something happened. You know, I knew I was no longer connected."

Not everyone is able to disconnect, as Crystal did. Nevertheless, you must recognize that when you and your former spouse divorced, you gave up the right to any involvement in his or her love life. If you haven't done it before, it is time to redefine your relationship with your children's stepparent and to focus on making this association as productive as possible.

Perhaps to accomplish this you need to reframe your thinking. Separate your anger with the stepparent from your children's needs, and then learn to deal with each separately. This may be especially hard, and important, when the stepparent was the "other man" or "other woman" in your ex's life while you were still married. Even harder yet is when this "interloper" was your friend, which happens so often that it is amazing how shocked we are if it happens to us.

The problem with holding on to resentment and bitterness toward someone who has hurt you is that it ties you into the past. Letting go of the anger frees you to move ahead with your life and your future. This doesn't mean that you have to condone behavior such as participation in extramarital affairs, but it does mean you must be willing to give up the concept you have of yourself as the injured party. Some people get so wrapped up in avenging themselves that they become controlled by their resentments. Some people get so engrossed in their efforts to prove to the world how mistreated they were by their former spouses and friends that they have taken on exaggerated attitudes of innocence and belief in their own angelical behavior—at the expense of their mental and emotional well-being. Sometimes giving up an image of yourself as the offended party can seem frightening; it is easier to do if you can accept that a stronger, healthier, happier self-image is waiting for you out there if you have the courage to rid yourself of your anger toward your ex's new spouse.

EXERCISE

To Whom It May Concern

For this exercise, you need a pencil, pen, or typewriter; some paper; and at least an hour or so without interruption.

1. Write a mock letter to your ex's new partner. Let your feelings rip. Write whatever you'd like to tell this person, no matter how explosive. Don't worry about punctuation or spelling. Just let your emotions fly onto the paper as satirically or straightforward as you want to. Don't worry about embarrassing yourself or hurting anyone else. Say what you feel.

2. Reread the letter several times. As you read, let your emotions flow. Don't hold back. If you want, set it aside (*out of sight and out of reach*) and come back to it the next day, and maybe the next. Each time you read it, it should have less impact on your emotions, and this process will desensitize you to your negative emotions.

3. When you're finished with the letter, *get rid* of it. If you feel like writing another letter, do so. But remember, these letters are for *your eyes only.*

You may also want to seek counseling to help you to work out your pain and anger. Keep in mind, however, that this process of expelling feelings of bitterness toward your ex's new partner is a *separate* issue from dealing with this person as your child's stepparent. Your anger and hurt at the "other man" or "other woman" are emotions that need to be put behind you. They belong only in your history. But the stepparent is a significant person in your child's present and future, and from this standpoint is also an important person in your life *now*.

Whether or not you *want* to communicate with your children's parallel stepparent, chances are the time will come when you *must*. You may have to reach your children about a sudden scheduling change for visitation, and the stepparent is the only one at home. Or you may get a phone call from the stepparent because your former spouse isn't home and your sick child is asking for you. It's very possible under these circumstances that the stepparent has done all he or she can do to take care of any immediate nursing duties, but a really sick child usually wants his or her mother or father, if only for reassurance. Don't assume this phone call means that the stepparent is incapable of handling the situation. It usually means that the stepparent is sensitive enough to your child's needs to want to do everything possible to make your child comfortable.

When talking with a counterpart stepparent, it is *safest* to remain neutral and emotionally uninvolved. Keep your focus on the issue at hand. If the call is about a sick child, get the details of the illness and then ask to speak with your child. Before hanging up, ask your child to get the stepparent back on the phone so you can discuss what you want him or her to do—and be sure to say thank you. If the call entails a scheduling change, a shift in activities, forgotten clothes, misplaced belongings, or whatever, stick to the subject. Be clear and concise, and as brief as politely possible.

Once you begin to appreciate the role of the stepparent in your child's life, you may want to begin to identify more closely with the stepparent in the role of counterpart parent. This means you will be more willing to consider the stepparent as a team player, working toward the goal of raising your child. It doesn't necessarily mean you will always agree with this person, but it does mean the two of you can begin to share some of your child's accomplishments, and some of his or her disappointments as well. You shouldn't have to agree on your children's mealtimes or homework study schedules in order to share a common concern about providing them with good nutrition and a good education.

You don't even have to like each other in order to function as parallel parents. This does not have to be a social relationship; it can be strictly pragmatic. You want your children to grow up in the most nurturing environment possible. Stepparents can add to your children's nurturing, and will be more apt to do so if they have a good relationship with the children. Your cooperative attitude toward the stepparent will affect your children's relationship with him or her in a positive way.

In communicating with your children's stepparent, there are some conversational guideposts that you may find useful. Perhaps the most obvious one is to *avoid unpleasant implications and sarcasm in your voice.* It is possible that your children's stepparent has already heard some unflattering comments about you from your ex, which is all the more reason for you to come across as a voice of reason and cooperation. It doesn't help, in setting up a pragmatic relationship with anyone, to show disagreeable or scornful traits.

Threats as a means of communication are not advisable when coexistence is the objective. Natural parents have the power (unless they have relinquished it), and power generally speaks for itself. When flaunted, however, it can cause resentment, so a gentle approach is often more useful.

If you are calling on the phone to speak with your former spouse or your child, and the stepparent answers, identify yourself politely and be pleasant. It is very rude to simply respond to a greeting with "Is Tommy there?" At the very least, say something like "Hello, [call the person by name]. This is Susan Smith. I'm calling to speak with Tommy. Is he available?" Of course, if you have begun to develop a relationship with the stepparent, you will carry on a brief conversation first, asking how the stepparent is and perhaps sharing a short piece of news about your child.

If you are calling to speak with the stepparent, and your child answers the phone, don't use him or her as a messenger. Children resent being used to deliver messages between parents or stepparents, because it makes them feel caught in the middle. Your message should be delivered directly to the stepparent.

If you are calling with disappointing news, be prepared to speak with the stepparent in case your children's other parent isn't available. Decide on what you are going to say before making the call so that you can be straightforward and concise. For example, if you must cancel parenting time at the last minute because of unforeseen circumstances, the news will be taken much better if it is delivered promptly and clearly. Try to be as empathetic as possible. Remember, it is likely that the stepparent's plans are being affected, just like everyone else's.

If your children's stepparent brings up issues that you would rather discuss with your ex, just say so in a polite fashion. You don't need to be apologetic about it, but assure the stepparent you are aware of his or her concern, and will discuss the matter with your ex as soon as possible. This approach not only helps lessen the chances of any misunderstandings between you and your ex, but it also helps keep the stepparent from being put in the middle of any disputes.

It's not a good idea to discuss personal matters about your ex with your children's stepparent. There are many reasons for this, including the possibility of misquotes or misunderstandings. Although it may be very tempting to agree that "he can be such a slob around the house," your relationship with your children's stepparent shouldn't be put in jeopardy over a discussion about the personality traits of your former spouse that are no longer your business. And if you suspect there's been a misunderstanding with your child's stepparent, address it immediately and straighten it out.

Try to remain flexible in finding solutions to situations of mutual interest. The best interests of your children can most often be served when the parents and stepparents act in an adaptable, cooperative manner.

When a child stops talking to a parent, a counterpart stepparent can act as a bridge in re-establishing the relationship. That was the case with Mike, his 16-year-old daughter, Gwen, and her stepfather, Andy. Gwen lived with Andy and her mother, and had weekly parenting time with her father. These times with her dad were very significant to her, and she considered his approval very important to her self-identity. When Gwen entered adolescence, she began putting on weight, particularly in her thighs. This trait ran in her father's family; many women in Mike's family were very thick through the thigh area. When his daughter began developing this trait, Mike started calling her by the nickname "Thunder-Thighs." This devastated Gwen. She became bulimic (a condition in which the sufferer attempts to control weight by vomiting). Fortunately, at the time her stepfather was making a film about bulimia, and picked up the symptoms immediately. The only way Andy could convince her to go to a psychologist was to promise that he'd never tell her father that she was sick. It was a financial hardship, because her medical insurance was under her father's policy, so Andy had to pay the medical bills out of his own pocket. Gwen recovered, par-tially because the bulimia was caught very, very early, but the treatment still took over a year. During this year, Gwen stopped talking to her father and cut off all communica-tion with him.

"During this whole period, I encouraged her to start a relationship with him again," Andy recounts, "which was probably the most difficult thing I have ever done in my life. It was very hard, in my mind, to justify what I was do-ing, and to convince Gwen that it was the right thing, when deep down I didn't want her to do it anyway. It would have been easier if there had been no relationship while she was living with her mother and me, but I knew she wasn't going to be living with us all her life, and eventually, she would resent what had happened and feel guilty about it, so I did it. It had to be done. And obviously it worked because Gwen accepted it; she only did it because her mother and I convinced her it was the right thing to do. It took a long time. It took over a year. Finally she estab-lished a relationship with him again."

Gwen is now a senior in college, and, interestingly enough, she chose to go into the same field as her father. When he offered her an internship with him this past summer, she took it, and enjoyed being with her father, one to one, for the first time in her life. It was exactly what she wanted. She's drawn much closer to him since then, and now their relationship is pretty solid. To this day Mike has no idea what Andy did to glue his and Gwen's rela-tionship back together.

Not only the adults can be sources of difficulty. Chil-dren can be opportunists, and it is not unusual for them to point out a stepparent's supposed permissiveness or generosity as a means of getting their own way. For ex-ample, they might say, "Nancy's so nice. If we don't make our beds in the morning, she spreads them up for us, and leaves little notes on our pillows that the leprechauns did it. Why don't you do that?" or "Why can't I use your golf clubs? Bill let me use his, and they cost a lot more than yours did." It's much easier for us to criticize Nancy for her undermining leniency or to malign Bill for his indulgence than to consider that our own children might be trying to manipulate us. However, even if you suspect that the stepparent's leniency is based more on a lack of interest than on any philosophical permissiveness, avoid making negative comments to this effect. These maligning comments are not productive, and can set the stage for children to create a running battle between their parents and stepparents. Instead of commenting to your children about their stepparent's behavior, use the situation as another chance to discuss alternative lifestyles and different approaches to child rearing. Although they may begin by telling you they prefer the stepparent's leniency, it will reassure your children that you are not manipulated by their comparisons and are accepting of their stepparent's behavior.

It is not unusual for stepparents with children of their own biological creation to show preferences for their natural children. It is, however, very difficult for the stepchildren to accept the inequity. Twenty-four-year-old Susan talks about her noncustodial stepmother: "I like her very much. She's a great woman. She is the reason my father kept in touch with my brother and me. She always forced him to get us on the weekends, especially when they were dating. She was great, you know, she always wanted us involved in what they were doing. But as her own daughters were born, and they've gotten older (they are now 18), she always makes sure that they get what they should from their father, the attention and everything. Once we got older, she never cared to do that for my brother and me."

Children notice even subtle differences where their stepsiblings are concerned. Susan laments, "There are pictures of the family around the house and that my stepmom carries in her wallet, and my brother and I aren't in them. But then there are other pictures of my brother and me, so there's different categories of what the family is at different times. And to my stepmom, to all her friends, the family is my two sisters and my dad and her, and they don't include my brother and me."

Nevertheless, Susan still loves her stepmother, and tries to look at the situation as objectively as possible. "In a sense, I don't blame her," she says, "because they are her natural children, and she wants to make sure that she's being a mother to them, just like my mother would do in any kind of circumstance."

As a natural parent, while watching your children being hurt by these subtle (and sometimes not so subtle) inequities, it can be a tall order to keep from showing anger. The most important thing to remember under these circumstances is that by showing your rage at a stepparent you may further damage the relationship between your children and their stepparent, creating an even more difficult situation with which your children must deal. A more appropriate approach is to concentrate on helping your kids to build their own self-esteem so that they can better weather unfairness by stepparents and others alike. This can be accomplished by your treating them with love, respect, and affection. Set aside special time for each one so that you can devote your undivided attention toward really listening to them and responding to their emotional needs. Give lots of hugs and recognition for trying. Acknowledge accomplishments, but be sure that you also validate your child for just being him- or herself.

You can also encourage your children to voice their bruised feelings to their stepparents in a frank, nonwhiny manner. For example, Susan's mother could have suggested that she express her unhappiness about the separate family pictures by saying, "I really like the picture of you and Dad and my sisters, and I would like to be in a family picture,

165

too. It hurts my feelings when I'm left out, because I like to be included as a part of the family." Often both step-parents and parents make inadvertent omissions that they'd be happy to correct if made aware of them. However, don't mislead your children by assuring them that the oversight will be corrected just because they draw it to their stepparent's attention. Instead, assure them that whether or not the inequity is corrected, they do have a right to make themselves heard on the subject.

In summary, children are entitled to have both natural parents involved in their lives, and this often means that stepparents may also become significant members of their families. Parents who keep involved with their children do not have to worry about losing a child's love to a step-parent, because children consider stepparents as additions to, rather than as replacements for, their mothers and fathers.

You will want to promote a positive relationship between your children and your counterpart stepparent because that person is going to be a significant person in your children's lives. It will be healthier and nicer for them if they can get along with that stepparent.

Children often suffer from feelings of disloyalty when a stepparent comes into their lives. With enough reassurances and consistent support from you, they can learn to feel more comfortable about establishing a positive relationship with their stepparent.

It is important for you to focus on your counterpart stepparent as a significant person in your children's lives, rather than as your adversary. In spite of the negative emotions that often plague the relationships of parents and parallel stepparents, often these counterpart parents collaborate to share the responsibilities of child raising. This can greatly reduce the stress children experience as a result of divorce and remarriage within their families.

▼

Chapter

8

Overcoming Well-Intentioned Advice

"I don't understand why you let him get away with it," Kathy's mother groans. "First he dumps you, and now, before the divorce is even final, he's exposing *your* children —*MY* grandchildren—to his new little hussy. If I were you . . . "

"I just heard your ex got a promotion," Lila's friend confides. "You better get him back into court and get your alimony raised before he starts making other commitments for that money."

"Listen, honey," June's sister urges, "I'd take him for everything he's got . . . or ever will have."

"How can you let your children be exposed to their mother's lover, and in the house that *you* bought and paid for?" Tom's father challenges. "You better take those kids away from her *now!*"

As you go into the divorce process, no matter how poorly or how well you think you might have adjusted or adapted to the situation, there will always be someone who will come along with your best interest at heart who can add grief, stress, and anxiety to the situation. Whether from well-meaning friends, parents, or in-laws, a brother, sister, neighbor, a co-worker or boss, there will be no shortage of advice. You'll get it right and left, from those who have "been through it themselves," from self-proclaimed experts who "just read somewhere . . . ," from someone who has been through "exactly what you are going through" (although no two situations are exactly alike). No matter how well you are adapting, be prepared to handle well-intentioned advice that can get you into trouble.

One of the first clear signs that advice is on its way is the phrase "Well, if I were you . . ." Once those words ring in your ears, *beware* of everything that comes after them. Finding reliable advice donors is never easy, and especially when you're facing such a traumatic change as divorce. During the divorce and its immediate aftermath, you are very vulnerable. Your emotions are raw. You may be feeling particularly insecure because of the newness and tenseness of the situation. And because of your susceptibility, you are not in the best frame of mind to sort out good advice from bad. Yet in spite of and because of your vulnerability, you'll get a barrage of unsolicited counsel. Some want to "save you from making the same mistakes they've made"; others want to share their experiences with you. There'll be the protectors and the vindicators; the avenging angels and the revengeful retaliators.

And you'll be tempted to rely on their counsel, because you'll be seeking information and guidance. When you're in unfamiliar territory, it's natural to gravitate toward those who seem to have knowledge of the terrain. You're going to be faced with a profusion of complicated decisions that affect not only you but your children as well.

This responsibility can seem overpowering, and trusted veterans' suggestions can be enticing. However, before you decide to rely on someone else's advice, assess its usefulness.

Begin by considering the source of the counsel. Evaluate the motives of the advice donors, and determine their objectivity. Other people's advice may be full of their own displaced hostility. Some advice givers may be trying to redeem their own failures by "helping you to do what is right." And some people get some conscious or unconscious pleasure out of helping to create pain for their acquaintances, and still others may have an ulterior motive behind their advice giving, such as personal gain. The first thing to consider is what kind of advisers these people have been to you, and others, in the past. If they've been ill intentioned, manipulative, and cynical, then probably they have not changed, and you should be on guard. As soon as you hear the phrase "Well, if I were you . . . ," *ignore* everything that comes after it. This is no time to give these people just one more chance, and possibly one more victim. Although they might have some useful information, it's too hard to sift out. Perhaps half the advice you get from these people will be useful. The problem is, which half?

But if these people have been unselfish, objective, and on target with their advice in the past, you can be more inclined to listen and evaluate further. However, past performance is still no guarantee of good advice. Cyn and Barbara had been dear friends ever since they'd moved into the same apartment complex the previous year. They were both divorced, and each had two children about the same ages. Cyn had been dating a kind, giving, successful veterinarian by the name of Larry for about six months, and when she told Barbara that she was considering calling it off, her friend reacted with disbelief. "You can't do that!" she exclaimed. "He's everything you always said you wanted in a stepfather for your children. He loves them. They love him. He always includes them in your activities together. I won't let you destroy your chances for happiness."

Cyn didn't know how to respond. She knew everything Barbara said was true. Larry was exactly what she'd thought she wanted as a husband, and as a stepfather for her children. Her kids adored him, and she felt they really needed a father figure in the household. There was only one problem: she didn't love Larry. And when she tried to convince herself that love wasn't everything, she had to admit to herself that, besides not loving him, he bored her.

"You're simply afraid of commitment," Barbara insisted. "And who could blame you? After being treated the way you were by your children's father, why wouldn't you be scared? You fear being rejected again, so you're doing the rejecting first. Just wait awhile until your confidence is built up. Once your self-esteem is stronger, you'll see that he's perfect for you and the kids."

Cyn knew that Barbara was a good friend and intended what was best for her, and so she put a lot of weight on her advice. She also felt guilty about her children's strong feelings for Larry, and didn't want to put them through another loss like they'd suffered in the divorce. Furthermore, Barbara had been right about the last man she'd dated, picking up on his philandering tendencies long before she herself had. Also, Cyn really *wanted* to believe Barbara. Barbara's contention that the relationship would bring security into Cyn's and the children's lives was hard to argue, so she continued to date Larry for several more unfulfilling months, extending false hopes to him about marriage and to her children about getting a stepfather.

Why had Barbara encouraged Cyn to keep dating someone she clearly didn't care for? To find the answer, it is necessary to look into the history of Barbara and Cyn's relationship. When the two had first met, neither had been dating anyone, and they'd shared many happy singles activities together. Then, Larry came into Cyn's life. Once Cyn and Larry had begun dating, Barbara felt suddenly set adrift by Cyn. She now had Friday and Saturday nights to fill by herself. It had taken her four months of aloneness before she'd met Jeff, and just when it looked like she and Cyn would again have a common ground to share, Cyn had announced she was bored with Larry and was dropping him. Barbara didn't want to lose her common ground with Cyn again, nor did she want Cyn to experience the loneliness she'd just escaped from. In addition, she was wrestling with her feelings about Jeff and his potential as a stepfather for her own children. In other words, Barbara's advice to Cyn may have been echoing what was happening in *her* life, not Cyn's.

When evaluating advice, ask yourself certain questions relating to the suggestions being proposed. The following offers you some criteria by which you can judge other's recommendations. Ask yourself

1. Does the advice promote mending fences between people?

2. Does the advice suggest a "win–win" situation for all involved?

3. Does the advice account for the feelings of all the parties involved?

4. Is the advice based on actual knowledge of *your* situation, or only some other "similar" situation?

5. Does the advice promote forgiveness, and yet at the same time allow for the honest expression of your disappointment, fear, and/or anger?

6. Is the advice honest, or does it rely on lies and deceit for its base?

7. Is the advice "fair" to all involved?

8. Is the advice reasonable to act on, or is it a tedious, complex process?

9. Does it "feel right" to you, not just in anger but at a time when you are more at peace with yourself?

10. Would you offer the same advice to someone you love?

It is very important to analyze your personal relationship with the person who is offering you advice. Often there is a tendency to follow advice unquestionably when its source is someone whom you greatly admire, or to dismiss it when it's from someone from whom you wish to establish your independence, such as a parent. It is also tempting, in this day of quick fixes and specialization, to put yourself blindly into the hands of "experts."

As the world has grown in its complexity, we have begun to put more and more emphasis on "expert advice." With technology growing at an ever faster rate, and each industry protecting its jurisdiction with ever-changing jargon for which it can charge consulting fees for translations of the secret language, society is moving away from self-reliance and toward an environment of advice seekers. We seek help in decision making on problems dealing with everything from personal finance to sexual pleasure; from how to choose a husband to how to choose a place setting. We have become so obsessed with the right credentials, the right schools, and the right references that we sometimes forget to use our own common sense in evaluating the advice we're paying for so dearly.

We have become so "expert oriented" that we sometimes look to the experts for advice outside their fields. We listen to movie stars to help us decide whom we should vote into public office. We're persuaded by rock stars about which soft drink we should buy. We look to politicians to advise us on health foods, and to television personalities to help us choose a long-distance telephone company. Is it any wonder, then, when we're so prone to accept the advice of "experts," that we often don't look for biases among our expert advisors?

One problem with seeking "expert" advice is our tendency to accept it blindly. For instance, throughout history people have sought advice from the clergy. It seems, at the very least, rude to question the authority of a religious professional. A judge once declared, when an attorney objected to a priest giving an opinion on a psychological evaluation, "If he isn't an expert in human relations, I don't know who is." But the priest had given no evidence of any formal training in psychology whatsoever. The priest, a Father Brown, was testifying in a case that involved a father seeking to bar his Protestant ex-wife from contact with their children.

The father, Julius, and his present wife, Margaret, had custody of the two girls, ages 10 and 12. Although Julius had fallen away from the Catholic church when he'd moved away from his parents' home and married the children's mother, Anne, he'd returned to it with a vengeance after his and Anne's divorce, and had subsequently married a young Catholic woman who held similar strong religious convictions. Julius and Margaret became very involved with their parish and with Father Brown, the parish priest.

Julius decided to create his ideal of the perfect "Catholic" family for Margaret and the two girls, so he set about to destroy any evidence of his former marriage. The problem was that the children's mother, Anne, wouldn't go away. No matter how he sabotaged parenting time between the girls and their mother, Anne stuck in there like glue. Anne's love for her children, and their love for her, made it unlikely that he could get them to avoid her. The children, feeling caught in their parents' battle, went to talk with Father Brown about their feelings.

Father Brown told the girls that although their natural mother, Anne, was their physical mother, Margaret was now their real mother, permanently, psychologically, socially, and security-wise. He also told them that their father, Julius, and Anne had "never been married."

When the children reported this back to their mother, Anne set up an appointment to talk with Father Brown herself. When confronted, he said that the girls must have misunderstood what he had meant. For instance, he said, he "meant" that the marriage of Julius and Anne had never been sanctioned by the Church, rather than that they'd never been legally married. Father Brown's explanation sounded reasonable to Anne until she asked to bring the children in and have him explain the "misunderstandings" to them. Father Brown flatly refused. He also told Anne that Julius was part of a family unit now and that he might need twenty-four hours of every day to solidify that family unit, thus leaving no time in the girls' lives for Anne. Furthermore, Father Brown told Anne that for the children to have two mothers attending a family affair would produce "a difficult situation." Difficult for whom, it was not clear.

Although it is not necessarily our intention to appraise the value of Father Brown's advice, much of it clearly contradicted the theme of this book, which is learning to share your children with your ex-spouse. Nevertheless, Father Brown's influence was felt by the judge deciding the case ("If he isn't an expert in human relationships, I don't know who is"), and led to Anne being denied parenting time for over a year until a higher court overturned his decision.

It is not unusual for clergy to focus on stabilizing those family members who stay in the congregation. During an interview for this book, a rabbi commented that in dealing with divorced parents, "You really have to stick with the parent who is a member of the synagogue. You

174

have to work with who's here, whether or not they would be your personal preferences between the parents." Clergy can often be invaluable as resources for sympathy, information, and understanding, but their religious background does not qualify them as "those who are never wrong or completely without prejudice."

A real problem with expert advice can emerge when the advice seeker turns over his or her own responsibility in the decision-making process to a "wizard," expecting that this person will produce miracles. In an age of expert overload, it's easy for us to welcome the foolproof methods offered by the professionals. We can become afraid to trust our own "inner experts." Deep down, most of us usually know what to do, but with our changing roles in a divorce situation, we often experience a sense of powerlessness and anxiety. These feelings of ineptness can lead us to consult strangers without considering that these counselors may have their own baggage of past influences or allegiances.

This phenomenon was demonstrated in the case of Dr. Herbert V, a certified clinical psychologist. Dr. V's specialty was psychometrics (the measurement of various psychological attributes such as IQ, attitudes, and so on) and statistics. His primary responsibility was teaching. His experiences included working as a consulting psychologist for several school districts and handling a part-time private practice that included, among other things, working with children. Dr. V was hired by a woman as an expert witness to make a psychological evaluation of her child, who was the center of a legal access battle.

The mother of the child was seeking to legally sever her son's relationship with his father, based on her perceptions of the father's behavior. For several years prior to this court case, the mother had kept parenting time by the father to a minimum, and had further sabotaged her son's relationship with his father by describing the father's

175

lifestyle as "bad." Dr. V had no access to this information, and did not dig it up through his information-gathering process.

Dr. V took a history of the situation from the mother, and then interviewed the child, Anthony, and gave him an IQ test. During the interview, Anthony described his mother in only "good" terms, and his father in only "bad" terms, just as his mother had taught him to do. In his evaluation of Anthony, Dr. V made several positive references to the "good" and "religious" upbringing that Anthony was getting from his mother. Basing his judgment on this one interview, Dr. V told the court that it would not be harmful for Anthony to have access with his father cut off.

On cross-examination, it became clear that Dr. V had no evidence about the behavior of Anthony's father, whom he had never met. Yet he told the court that the man's behavior needed to be "changed." In self-contradiction, he admitted that the alleged "bad" behavior Anthony described in his father was "well within the acceptable mores of our society." He also testified that Anthony's upbringing by his mother "would tend not to be tolerant of other lifestyles." In his summary, he noted that Anthony had supposedly described his mother's behavior as "moral." But under cross-examination he admitted, "I think this could be my interpretation from what [Anthony] said because he described *what to me* are morals regarding drinking, smoking and going to church and so on and so forth."

Dr. V's credentials included training as a minister of the Church of the Nazarene. He had been a lay minister for many years, and had been a pastor as well. This background may well have been reflected in his evaluation of Anthony's mother's behavior as being moral, and as Anthony's father's behavior as needing to be changed. When challenged on his report by another expert witness, Dr. V wrote a supplement to his evaluation. As a basis for his report, he phoned Anthony's mother's attorney and discussed the whole situation with him, including what the lawyer thought should be written in the report, rather than relying on his own professional opinion.

Whether or not Dr. V's intentions were good, his advice to the court came distorted with moral judgments. This is the kind of prejudicial baggage that advice seekers need to beware of in considering sources of expert counsel.

It is extremely important to shop around for qualified, reputable counseling. A professional woman in her forties, Anita, relates her experiences with seeking expert help. "My ex-husband left me very abruptly," she says. "After twenty-three years of marriage, he left me a note. It was a total shock to me. My young son was 10 years old at the time. I was in this total depression. I told everybody at the time I felt like I had a bowling ball in the middle of my stomach. I lost thirty-five pounds in five weeks. I sought counseling.

"I was seeing a counselor at the local Presbyterian Church—the assistant minister. Everyone of us who went into that group eventually got divorced, and the counselor ran off with one of the patient's wives.

"After he left, one of the men from the group recommended another counselor in town. I went to her for a while but I wasn't getting very far with her. I wasn't happy. I didn't really like her, and didn't have anything to say to her. Now, I needed *help*. Unfortunately I wasn't smart enough to say to her, 'Can you recommend someone else? I really don't think we're getting anywhere.' Not long after that, she put on a long dress and long beads and went off with one of *her* patients and became a Moonie or something. And she was a married woman with two children.

"I didn't seek out anyone else for awhile. The way I handled it at the time was to run. That initial experience, when I needed them *so badly*, was *devastating*."

Fortunately, there are unbiased, knowledgeable counselors out there who are qualified to help you sort out your issues. The problem arises when advice seekers blindly accept certificates and credentials as evidence of competence without investigating the expert's common sense and objectivity, and without checking his or her references from others who have been counseled. The key is to look for someone who teaches you how to *solve your own problems,* rather than for someone who provides you with all the answers. If you suspect you're seeing the wrong counselor, you probably are.

Now, it isn't just advice from "experts" that can lead you astray, and free advice is often more bountiful than that you pay for. Frequently what motivates your friends and relatives to offer advice is truly their affection for you and their desire to help, ill advised though it may be. For the most part, these people really don't know that their advice can be causing you more problems than help.

One killer clue to advice you might want to ignore is prefaced by the phrase, "Well, if they were my kids . . ." It seems that people are often driven to offer advice about "how you should raise your children." A further signal that you might want to ignore these advisors is when they begin a long recitation about how they handled their own children under the "same" circumstances, or how their sister handled her children, or how the neighbors handled their children. It's awesome, how much personal advice flows about how others ought to behave. When you get this advice, grant the donor the benefit of the doubt. Ask yourself if you can learn anything from the information by example or by exception (that is, learn from other's mistakes). If not, disregard it. Don't blame the well-intentioned advisors, but take what they have to say with a grain of salt, and when necessary, pull the plug on them.

It can be very difficult for extended-family members to accept that for your children to maintain a frequent and meaningful relationship with their other parent is in their best interest. Especially for your parents, who may have watched helplessly as you suffered through the divorce, it can be hard not to bad-mouth your ex to you. Many older family members have had little or no experience in coping with the aftermath of divorce, and they are apt to see it as a battle in which sides must be taken. They may be very angry at your children's other parent, and are apt to vent their anger in front of you, encouraging you to join in their bitter outbursts. Their intentions may be to demonstrate their loyalty to you by denouncing your children's other parent.

The most productive thing you can do is to confront the issue directly. Explain that while you appreciate their loyalty toward you, you are working toward a coparenting relationship with your former spouse, and that it is not helpful to be reminded of past grievances. Reassure them that you love them, and ask for their help in not stirring up old issues. Ask for advice on how to make peace, not war.

This could also be a good time to ask them not to speak disparagingly of your former spouse to your children. Often children look to a grandparent as an objective party in whom they can confide, and when that grandparent says negative things about one of their parents, it can erode the children's sense of stability if they have to discount that grandparent as biased. Remind your parents that when they make nasty remarks or insinuations to your children about their other parent, the children will feel torn between loyalty to their parent and loyalty to their grandparents. Such a conflict will only intensify their sadness. Suggest to them that negative remarks about your ex to your children might backfire. Point out that when children's loyalty to their other parent is strong, the children will be apt to write off the grandparents. Assure your parents that this would be very upsetting to you.

Your children's grandparents are not the only ones apt to fuel the fires of your discontent. Anyone important within your social structure who is not aware of your intentions to work toward a coparenting relationship with your former spouse may try to keep the conflict between you two alive. Friends, as well as family, need to hear your views on your intentions to redefine your relationship with your children's other parent. Often the best approach is to ask for their support in your efforts. People are more apt to take a positive role in a situation when they feel informed and involved with its implementation. You might also explain the tactics you intend to use in creating this positive relationship with your children's other parent.

Although friendship is the motivator for some advice donors, another inducement that people have for offering suggestions on other people's behavior is that it gives them the chance to continue, vicariously, some ongoing unfinished business of their own. This motivation is often unconscious, but it can nevertheless lead to negative consequences. Take, for instance, the case of 35-year-old June. Recently divorced, and having gone through a terrible custody battle, she is ever anxious to share her advice with her friend, Alice, who is negotiating with her husband on a divorce settlement. "If I were you," she cautions, "I wouldn't let the SOB near those children. When my ex-husband asked me to let him take our children to his mother's, I agreed. Then he used it against me in court, contending that I sent the children to her in order to escape responsibility for them. I should never have buckled under and let him take the kids. What did it get me? A lot of heartache and misery, that's what I got. I tried to be fair, and he used it against me in a custody fight. Don't let your husband get the jump on you. Go for the jugular. Get him before he gets you. Get in the first strike and let him know that you're one to be reckoned with."

Here is a bitter, angry person who has not resolved her own discontent with her circumstances, and is now suggesting vehemently that her best friend act aggressively and quickly against her husband. June's feelings are sincere and her intentions are pure, but she is agitating a possibly otherwise amiable situation. She is trying to help her friend avoid the pain and misery she has experienced, and she is also vicariously avenging herself. June is trying to right a wrong that has nothing to do with Alice or her circumstances. In such situations, nobody intends to do harm, but harm can be the outcome.

Of course, some advice donors among your acquaintances may go out of their way to make your life more miserable. These people may have it out for you, or for your former spouse, or they may be among those who thrive on causing trouble. In any case, *beware* of anyone bringing you news about the goings-on of your former spouse. Here are some examples of tidbits to ignore:

- "I hear your ex is going to Vail to ski. I thought you said he was late with his child support payments?"
- "I ran into Susie the other day. She tells me your ex says he's still in love with you."
- "I hear your ex just bought a new fur coat. Is that how she spends your child support money?"
- "I met your ex's new flame. Did he give her that rock she wears on her left hand?"
- "You're not going to let the kids spend Christmas with *her*, are you?"

These statements, and comments like them, come under the heading of meddling. They are usually unsolicited

181

and have as their main objective to keep your emotions tender and your anger hot. The advice donor hopes to keep the pressure on for you to start the old fight again with your former spouse. When you receive such unsolicited advice, *ignore* it. Especially if you are vulnerable to suggestions of others because you tend toward dependency or compliancy, stay aware of the motives behind the unsought advice, because you're likely to be influenced by it. When you're accosted by such voluntary opinions, inform the donors that, while you appreciate the help they may have offered in the past, thanks to the strong support you've received you now feel self-reliant enough to move on in your life without their further counsel.

So where does that leave you? You're hurt, scared, and confused; your guts tell you that you want to hurt back and get even, but your head is telling you differently. You are getting all kinds of suggestions, but you don't know how to separate the good from the bad. How do you evaluate the essence of the advice?

To begin with, *the best advice doesn't tell you what to do, but instead it helps you to sort out your options.* When evaluating different options, a good technique is to keep a journal and write down the advice you receive. For each entry, ask yourself,

- Is this consistent with the outcome that I really want?
- Will this get me what is best for me and for the children?

If it is not, then cross it out. If the advice has some merit, then ask yourself these questions:

- What are my options?
- Do I need to expand my information base before making a decision?

- Have I given this enough thought?
- What have others told me?
- What do I want to come from all this?
- What steps must I take to get me what I want?

Once you've answered these questions, it can be useful to find people you trust to act as sounding boards for your thoughts. One place you might look is to members of support groups or advocacy groups in your community. Look for people who are willing to help you evaluate various strategies for fulfilling each of your goals, rather than for those who insist on telling you what to do. Look for those who keep confidences and avoid gossiping about mutual acquaintances. When a potential advisor asks a lot of questions about what outcome you want, it's usually a good indication that he or she is trying to understand the situation as it affects *you* rather than him- or herself.

The best advice usually echoes your own intuition. Most people are capable of making decisions that best suit their needs. Sometimes the fear of making mistakes or looking foolish can blur an individual's self-confidence in his or her ability to make a good decision, but each time you accept advice blindly you take a step away from self-reliance.

If you still don't feel comfortable in choosing between your options, seek an unbiased, knowledgeable third party; someone who understands the dynamics of peacemaking and the pitfalls of divorcing relationships. That person is most often a trained and reputable counselor educated to help *you* sort out issues you legitimately "own" from issues suggested by well-intentioned onlookers. If you find that what you're being offered by this "expert" is an excuse to do nothing, or a way to blame others for your actions, or a set of moral judgments and prejudices, then it's time to look for another counselor, because in the final analysis you will be living with the consequences. That final decision is always yours, and a good counselor is one who will help you form your own resolutions.

Distinguishing other people's good advice from bad can be a challenge, but what do you do if you find that *you* are the well-intentioned advisor? Often we find ourselves wanting to offer advice or counsel to our friends and relatives about some aspect of their lives. There is no greater flattery than to have someone ask, "Can you help me? I've got a problem, and I believe you can help." These solicitations for advice can stroke our egos because they say to us, "You are wise and talented. You can help others. You have the ability to heal pain. You're smart and I need some of your wisdom." We can all be duped by this adulation. We are taught from childhood by our families and our churches that it is our duty to help our fellows, and so we get sucked in.

To avoid jumping in "where more experienced folks fear to tread," there's an excellent technique for being kind and compassionate and helpful without doing damage. First, ask the advice seeker, "Whom else have you asked for help?" Chances are this person has asked other people the same questions and is comparing answers. If this is the case, follow up with "What advice did they give you?"

If everyone's advice is consistent, you can say something like "It seems that there is a consensus of opinion, but for some reason you don't seem to feel comfortable or convinced because if you did, you wouldn't be asking me. Tell me what you really want to do in this situation." This helps the person get in touch with his or her own wants and needs. If you can't agree with your friend, you can say something to the effect of "These are difficult situations, and you may get lots of conflicting advice. You are one of my best friends, and I don't really feel I can be objective here. I'm tempted to tell you what you want to hear, because I want you to know that I support you, but the best support I can give you, because I care about you, is to suggest that you consult an objective professional who is capable of helping you sort out the issues. If you'd like, I'd be happy to help you find one who's reputable."

Giving advice is always a losing proposition. No matter what you advise, someone else may offer a conflicting or contrary suggestion, and the situation will become polarized. Suddenly sides are formed, and without knowing it you are categorized into one of the "camps" of opinion, none of which may be in the person's best interest.

It's hard to keep our opinions to ourselves when someone we care about is in emotional pain. The problem is that how we would deal with a situation is often not best for someone else—just as your prescription medicine may relieve your headache, but may cause hypertension in your best friend. We are being asked how we would deal with someone else's problem, and this can create a whole new set of issues for the advice seeker. Although it may *seem* our approach to our own recent visitation problems would be useful to someone facing a similar set of circumstances, our successful approach may have devastating results for that other person.

Sometimes what an advice seeker needs most is a listener. Often, if you just let your friends express themselves while you keep your opinions to yourself, they can come up with their own solutions. If you can offer compassion and empathy rather than answers, you will be helping them reaffirm their own self-reliance while allowing them the dignity of dealing with their own lives.

In summary, as you go through the divorce process, there will be no shortage of advice donors. This advice, no matter how well intentioned, can add grief, stress, and anxiety to the process.

Most often, the majority of advice donors have the best of intentions at heart. However, some need to continue vicariously some ongoing, unfinished fight of their own, or really do want to make your life more miserable. In any case, *beware* of unsolicited advice. It's usually best ignored.

In this day of expert overload, society is moving away from self-reliance and toward advice seekers. It is wise to avoid putting yourself blindly into the hands of professional counselors. The key to finding a knowledgeable therapist is to look for someone who teaches you to solve your own problems, rather than for someone who gives you all the answers. If you think you're seeing the wrong counselor, you probably are.

Friends and family alike need to hear your intentions to share your children with their other parent. Otherwise, they may try to keep the conflict between you and your former spouse alive.

The best advice doesn't tell you what to do, but instead helps you sort out your own options. The techniques discussed in this chapter can help you in this process.

And the best advice for giving advice is *don't*.

Chapter

9

The Children Speak

"**W**ell, the first thing that comes to mind about being the child of divorced parents is always being in the middle between your parents," said 25-year-old Andrea, whose parents were divorced when she was 3. "Always. Being, you know, alone. Oh, god, it puts you in the middle. They want you to go against the other one all the time. That's always the hardest thing." The slight, sandy-haired young woman sighed as she gazed out the window of her tiny Los Angeles apartment. She continued, "I just think that divorced parents need to—I hate to say 'grow up'—but they *do* need to grow up and talk to each other . . . put their differences aside for just a little while."

Andrea is one of the dozens of young people who talked with us in depth concerning their feelings about being the children of divorced parents. Ranging in ages from 10 to 30, they represented a wide cross section of parental harmony and discord. They were living in different parts of the country, including the Northeast, Southeast, Midwest, and West Coast. Some of them were so young when their parents divorced that they have no defined memories of life within their original nuclear families; others ranged in ages from 2 to 20 when their parents separated. Yet they all shared a willingness to talk to us in the hope that their input might help shape the future of divorced parenting and thus alleviate some of the pain for other children of divorce.

Some of these young people were relieved when their parents finally divorced. They hoped it would mean the fighting would stop. Others were surprised and shocked to learn that their parents were separating. Still others were devastated by the news of the impending split-up. Whatever their perspectives on the divorce itself, certain common concerns emerged from the discussions that suggested areas on which divorcing parents should concentrate.

The first of these had to do with the announcement and explanation of the divorce itself. In listening to the children of divorce, we found it poignantly clear that although children may understand their parents will no longer be living together, they have no way of gauging what effect the divorce will have on them. The explanations may seem very clear to us as adults. For our children, who are facing a traumatic change for which they have no frame of reference, the same explanations can be totally confusing.

Take Megan, a reserved 15-year-old high school sophomore whose parents divorced when she was 7. "I didn't really realize what was going on," she began. "I thought, when my dad was moving out, I kind of thought we were going on a vacation." She blushed, self-consciously laughed at herself, and then continued, "I mean, because he was moving his stuff out and everything. I didn't understand."

Gloria, a lively young woman with a cheerful smile, was 9 years old when her parents separated. She described her perception of what was happening at the time: "It was confusing. My parents just told me that it wasn't my fault; that they were having trouble and needed time away from each other to think things out. I was real young, and I was just real confused by everything. I didn't really understand. It was confusing because I remember going to a different place to see my dad, a different town, and I didn't understand why he was there instead of at home. I didn't *want* to understand, so I'd pretend that everything was OK; that Dad just wasn't home for a little while, but he'd be back. You know, he'd be back shortly." She paused, then added with a cheerless laugh, "I thought."

Many young people told us they took the blame for their parents' divorce. One such young man, David, was 13 when his parents separated. Now a 24-year-old social worker in the Southeast, David discussed the frustration he felt as a teenager trying to "fix" his parents' relationship. "My sisters and I thought the divorce was our fault, and we wanted to get them back together. As kids we were always fighting, you know, and so we tried to get along so we could get them back together." The friendly redhead fidgeted with the signet ring he wore on his right hand as he spoke. "We couldn't even consider the fact that my dad would actually leave, or that the word *divorce* really meant that my parents weren't going to be together anymore, so we spent all our time trying to patch them up." David's voice took on a tone of finality as he concluded, "And then, all of a sudden, my dad was gone, and it was just harsh reality."

Fifteen-year-old Megan told us, "I guess I thought it was my fault for a little while. I used to send cards through the mail, like on their anniversary, trying to get them back together. I don't know—mostly I was so little I didn't understand. I kind of thought that they would get back together."

Whatever their ages or perceptions of divorce, children are deeply affected by the departure of one parent from their home. "It's the strangest thing," said one young man whose father moved out of the family home when the boy was barely 3 years old. "The only memory I have in this house with my dad is of the day he left. I remember it vividly. My mom and sister and I standing outside; it was snowing, and I remember my dad backing out of the driveway. The three of us, standing on the stoop with the snow blowing all around us, and he's backing out of the driveway."

"If they could have *explained* to us what was going on instead of my dad just disappearing," said another young man who recently received his teaching degree from a university in the Midwest. "Parents need to reassure their children that they're not the cause of the divorce. And they should make things as comfortable as possible for the children. In my case my dad disappeared for a month, and then after that there was years worth of fighting. All those eruptions." The 25-year-old ran his fingers through his blond hair. He continued, "I think the children should be the primary focus in a divorce—not the divorcing people. The parents have to save the children, because it's the children who have their whole lives ahead of them. The two people divorcing—they're going through tough times, but their lives are set. Their personalities have already been developed. But their children need a chance. If the parents screw them over with their fighting and hostility, the impact is tremendous, so I think parents should focus on the children."

Another issue that seemed to crop up time and again was that of financial disputes. "Tell your father I need money," was a recurring mission that many of these children grew up with. Take Melinda, a blue-eyed teenager from the Northeast who is presently attending college. "My mom would say, 'He owes me alimony,' and I would have to tell my dad. Then he would say, 'No, I'm not giving it to her,' or 'No, I already paid her,' and I would have to go back and tell her that. I'd be *livid*. You know, I'd be stuck in the middle. Even to this day, like when I had my wisdom teeth out this summer, my mom said, 'You know, your father could help pay. Tell him it'd be nice to know if he'd help me on this,' and I told him, and he said, 'No.'"

Melinda continued, "My mother thinks she got cheated or something in the divorce; that she didn't get what she deserved. I say, 'Mom, just forget about it.' I mean, after a while it's annoying. You don't even want to bring up your father or mention anything about him because you don't want to hear about the money."

Whatever the financial arrangements were between the parents of the young people we interviewed, it became clear that the children did not want the responsibility of acting as a collection agency for child support payments. Even when the delinquent parent willingly gave the money to the child, the child resented having to ask for it. Although recently some have advocated that children be required to ask for child support payments before being allowed to see their other parent, we agree with the young people we interviewed that child support payments are a grown-up issue, and should be handled by the parents without asking the children to intercede, or even to take part in cooperating. These are not kid issues. Withholding access of a child to his or her other parent because of a money issue puts the child smack in the middle of the money fight. It also gives the implicit message that relationships are about money, not love. It is *not* the child's responsibility to put food on the table, and the child should not be used as ransom to collect for the house payments.

Yet loving relationships with children do not exclude accepting both physical and financial responsibility for their needs. Children require and deserve the basic necessities of life. When both parents take on the financial and physical responsibility to provide for these needs, they set a good example for their children of how to behave like responsible adults. New obligations such as a current spouse or more children don't negate in any way a prior responsibility to children from a former marriage. One young person who had had weekly time with her dad and stepmother during her growing-up years told us, "I would have felt more a part of my dad's family if he'd offered my brother and me [from a former marriage] the same things he offered my sisters and younger brother [from his present marriage], which he never did. When my brother and I were in high school, we had to work every summer saving money for college. My sisters and younger brother never had to do that. They always went away to summer camp—a sailing camp down in Virginia somewhere. We were never offered the same things. Not that I would have even wanted to go to sailing camp, but I would have liked to be given the chance if I'd wanted to."

Often, noncustodial supporting parents get so caught up in their resentments at having to pay money to their former spouses that they lose sight of the purpose of the payments: *to provide for their children.* It only makes the situation worse when the parents receiving the money treat the payments as some kind of payoff for their own emotional injuries suffered or as retribution for having been left. It is important that both parents understand the purpose of child support and *focus on the children and their emotional and financial needs.*

Jackie, a 22-year-old artists' representative from the West Coast, said that she often had to ask for her own child support. "If I was going over to my dad's, my mom would say, 'Well, make sure you get the child support check.' It would have been much more comfortable if they'd have handled it without involving me! Anything that I didn't have to do that related to the two of them interchanging was always easier."

Child support payments are odd in that they often make up a large percentage of the income of the paying person, and yet they make a very small contribution toward the children's financial necessities. It can help for the paying parent to look at the budget of a receiving parent, to see where "all the money goes." It's very easy to forget how much it costs to feed, clothe, and shelter children in today's economy. Just because a court doesn't require the paying parent to see where the child support money goes, it can make a parent a lot more willing to pay when he or she can see in black and white that the money is being spent to meet the needs of the children. Writing the checks can also seem less galling for the paying parent when he or she writes the children's names on the memo line of the check (that is, for Suzy and Johnny). Some paying parents find the process easier when they have their banks or employers or accountants make the payments automatically each month so that they don't have to personally think about it on a regular basis.

If you are a custodial parent who receives child support payments, and find that your children are constantly asking you for things you can't afford, don't be quick to blame your lowly financial status on your meager child support payments. These circumstances present good occasions to discuss with your children the ramifications of the choices we all make in life. For example, if you had decided to marry later and get a good, solid education first, you might now be in a better position to contribute more to your family's financial situation. Or, if you had decided to work during your marriage rather than to become financially dependent on your former spouse's income, then you would already be established in a career, and would not have to face reentry into the job market. And while you may have made these choices in order to be home with your children, the point here is that *you* made the choices. To exclude these choices from your explanation as to why Johnny can't have a new baseball mitt denies him complete access to the whole picture. Although it may be tempting to put all the blame for your reduced financial status on Johnny's other parent, it is healthier for Johnny to see you sharing in the responsibility for him and for yourself. Once you accept that you are fully responsible for yourself, then it will become easier for you to stop blaming your child's other parent for your situation.

However, if Suzy wants a new tennis racquet, and you as the custodial, receiving parent can't afford to buy her one, it's OK to suggest that Suzy might ask her other parent for it. You could say something like "It simply doesn't fit into the budget, Suzy, but perhaps your mother [or father] could help you out with this one." However, don't insinuate that it's the other parent's responsibility to buy it for her. Remember, even when you were married to your former spouse, the two of you probably couldn't afford to buy Suzy everything she wanted. Besides, even if your child's other parent could afford to buy the tennis racquet, but chooses not to, it doesn't do your child any good to hear you make negative remarks about that. It might also be helpful if you let your ex know the request is coming, and why. You might say, "Suzy needs a new tennis racquet, and there's not enough money this month to buy it for her. I suggested that she might ask you for it, and I wanted you to know." If your ex does not buy Suzy the racquet, then she'll have to do without it. She may be disappointed, but at least she won't feel that she's been responsible for yet another fight between her parents.

Perhaps surprisingly, none of the children of divorce that we interviewed saw the financial disparity between their parents as a negative or positive reflection on either parent. Because stories of divorce so often emphasize the father who leaves home and then showers the children with gifts while the mother can barely make ends meet, we expected to hear stories about extravagant gifts from noncustodial parents. This was not the case. Although some of the young people acknowledged having received expensive gifts from their noncustodial parents as they were

194

growing up, they seemed to put no more or less value on these gifts than they did on the less extravagant gifts they received from their other parents. This suggests that there is no need to take nice things away from kids, or to put restrictions on how often they can be used or played with or worn, for fear of ruining a child's value system. Only when the other parent complained about not being able to compete did the financial disparity became an issue to the child. "At times, my mother says things like 'Oh, he's got the money to take you away to nice places and I don't,'" said one first-year college student. "It makes you feel like she's always worried about money and paying bills, and when I'm with my dad I don't have to worry about anything. Everything's happy."

Although presents were not a big issue to these children of divorce, holidays were. "The first thing I thought about after my parents' divorce was whom I'd spend the holidays with and stuff like that," said one 10-year-old child from the Midwest.

"To this day, Christmas is still a battle," lamented a 20-year-old from the Southeast. "I mean, it's supposed to switch every year. Next year I'd be with my dad 'cause I was with my mom this year. It's like they both *want* you, and you feel so *torn* between them. It's like, which way do I go? Because there's still more arguing to come. Lots more."

"Holidays kind of depress me," said a 24-year-old male student from the Northeast. "Not to a point where I'm an emotional wreck or anything, but still, it gets to me. It's been eleven years since my parents' divorce, and still, every time my sisters and I have a Thanksgiving or Christmas at my mom's, it's like there's an absence with my dad gone, and no one has any fun. It's strange. When I'm over at my mom's house I think about my dad. She does too, in a negative way. She doesn't like him at all."

"Holidays are the worst," said yet another young college student, "because that's when weird things come into it. Definitely. It's then that you feel, 'Gotta be with Mom.' 'Gotta be with Dad.' This year was better, because my dad was with a friend, but I can remember one Christmas Eve when I was with my mom and brother at my grandparents, and I knew Dad was home alone so I called to wish him a happy Christmas Eve. I felt *so* bad and *so* guilty. Here I was with all these people, and he was home alone. I got so upset. I wanted to be with him, but I couldn't, because technically it was Mother's year. It wasn't my fault, but I felt guilty. And I really shouldn't have, but I did." She laughed a hollow little laugh and rolled her eyes.

"I hoped that one day my parents would be friends," she continued. "And talk to each other like human beings. For example, my boyfriend's parents really shocked me. I went to his house for Thanksgiving dinner to meet his family for the first time. His mom and stepfather were there. And his real father and his girlfriend were there. Everybody was there." She dropped her voice to a whisper. "And I said, 'Your mother and father are here together? I could never put my parents in the same room together.'" She raised her voice again. "It just *blows* my mind. It's like *wow*. So I always kind of hoped *my* parents would be like that. You know, 'Let's stop arguing.'"

(We found the scenario of the divorced parents spending the holidays together so intriguing that we interviewed the young man and his mother. Excerpts from those interviews are included in Chapter 11.)

Many of the young people we spoke with voiced an opinion on the effect their parents' divorce might have on their own decisions of whether or not to marry. Ten-year-old Candy told us, "If a boy asks me to marry him or something, I think I would wait awhile to see if I really do like him. I'd like to live together before I got married to see if we were really going to get along and agree on stuff."

Twenty-year-old Gloria said her parents are still fighting after four separations and a divorce. "The thought of marriage scares me. It scares me a *lot* to think about it. And at times, I'll envision myself with kids or something, and I just see myself. I see no husband. I think that's partly because I grew up in a divorced family. It scares me because I'm always asking myself, 'Well, will I get divorced? Will I have kids? What will I put them through?' And you always say you don't want to put your kids through what *you* went through—which I *don't*. I never want to have my kids go through a divorce situation. I think it makes you *real* hesitant toward marriage."

In spite of a real concern about making a matrimonial commitment, however, most of the young people we spoke with said they would consider divorce if they found themselves in an unhappy marriage. Ten-year-old Candy told us, "I don't think people should stay together if they don't like each other." Fifteen-year-old Megan said, "I think I'd probably get a divorce. Even if I had kids, and I knew it would hurt, I wouldn't be able to go on living my life in a miserable situation. If you're miserable, then everybody'll know it pretty soon. Your kids will pick up on it, anyway, so I'd probably get a divorce." Megan's parents have managed to communicate with each other and work together in a positive coparenting relationship.

The children of divorce whose parents have kept the battle going over the years made it clear to us that, while they might divorce, they would try to deal with it better than their parents had. "If I ever married and got divorced," said 25-year-old Andrea, "I'm sure I'd do it in a different manner than my parents did. If I could, I'd make sure I stayed friends with my ex-husband, you know. I'd make sure that it wasn't a messy, terrible divorce— especially if there were children involved."

These young people didn't seem to resent their parents' decision to divorce. Sixteen-year-old Scott expressed his feelings this way: "If they hadn't gotten a divorce, I think it [home] would have been an unhappy place to be. I just don't think it would have been a good environment to be around. I mean, I'm glad now," he paused and snickered, "not like happy or anything, that they got a divorce, but I'm glad, because I know that it's for the best. I mean, if I could go back and somehow change it so that they would still get along, then I would, because that would have been nice. If they could have gotten along and everything. If they couldn't, it would be miserable."

"I was never one of those kids who thought, 'Oh, I hope they get back together,'" said another teenager. "I never wanted that, because it would be more anger and more fighting, and I just didn't want that. When they were together, they argued. I mean, what fun is it to be with parents who argue all the time?"

Although these young people didn't seem to resent their parents' divorces, they did show anger and sadness over the anger their parents showed toward each other. "If I could change one thing about my childhood," said one particularly articulate young woman, "I'd take away all my memories of my parents fighting. I'd just erase all the pain—the screaming—lots of arguing. Like when they were going to court, my dad got nasty. He brought up accusations that my mother used to come home drunk, or he'd take pictures of the refrigerator with no food in it. He was trying to get custody of my brother and me and prove that she was an unfit mother, and I just thought, 'Why is he doing this?' because she *wasn't* an unfit mother. Then she got nasty, and toward the end they were doing anything and everything against each other to win us. I thought, if this is what it's going to be like, neither of them should have us. You know, this shouldn't be a fight for your children. I'd like to take away the pain, but I don't think you can. You can't take it away. . . ."

"I lived with my dad after my parents were divorced," said a sensitive young man, "and my mom and dad didn't get along at all. I tried to carry my dad's emotions with me. I thought that if I could feel bitter toward my mom, I was doing it for my dad, because I *knew* he felt very negative toward my mom. It made it a lot harder for me to have a relationship with my mom. It hurt the relation-ship with my mom tremendously. I didn't see her much at all. Because of that I'll never again think of her as my *mom*—a person I can go to like I used to. She always used to be there for me. My dad was just kind of there. I re-member she'd always comfort me whenever I was nervous about something or felt an emotional need. Since then I've lost the idea of 'mother' and a sense of family. I lost that."

"I can remember my dad, after the divorce, referring to my mother as 'the bitch,'" a young woman told us. "He'd always say 'the bitch.' It made me *angry,* because that was my *mother.* It was my *mother* he was talking about."

"Parents can play head games with you," declared one political science major. "For instance, when you go visit one parent, and the parent you live with doesn't want to hear anything good about the visit, the children *know* that. As a child, you go back home and you *fake* a bad time, or you really do have a crummy time with your other parent because the parent you're living with wants you to have a crummy time. They don't like that person you're going to see. It can totally screw up your thinking."

Big events for these children of quarreling divorced parents were an ever-present threat. "You always anticipate what they're going to do," said one recent high school graduate, "and it ruins your day. All through graduation, and afterward, I was so worried about them and what was going to happen and who was going to say what and who was going to start a fight, that it ruined things. You just wish that they would relax, so that *you* can. I think it'd be a lot easier if parents got along better, because it'd make things so much easier for kids and for everybody else."

"I think about things like if I ever got married," said the daughter of two dueling parents. "The wedding, you know, if they were all at the wedding together. You think about the littlest things. You don't think about what your dress is going to look like, or walking down the aisle straight, or if you're going to trip. You just worry about what your parents are going to do. Why can't they just grow up and be like, 'OK, this is no big deal'? I hope by the time I get married that they'll both be at points in their lives where they're happy, and that the bitterness will be behind them."

"I just wanted it to be a perfect day," Gloria told us about her graduation. "I think that I was more uptight than anyone else there. I didn't know what to talk about. What to say. I didn't want to *offend* anyone. I didn't want to get in the middle. I didn't want to start a fight. I just wanted everything to go right. I just felt it was *my* day and that no one should fight.

"My father gave me a big dinner afterward for some of my really close friends. He wouldn't invite my mom or my grandfather. I wanted my mother there but he said, 'No, this is a gift to you and I want to give you this little party and I don't think she needs to be there.' I thought it was important that she be there because they were both my parents, and it was *my* graduation, and I couldn't understand why they couldn't share it together. I accepted it, but I didn't like it, because I wanted her to be there. I thought about her while I was at the dinner. I made it through. It was just that I felt I hurt her in a way. Or I'd have hurt my dad in another way if I did bring her. So you're sort of stuck at both ends—between a rock and a hard place, as they say."

There were those whose parents worked at coparenting and were successful enough at it to attend the same events without causing their children stress. "It's nice" said one such teenager, "even though they're not involved together anymore. They're still both important to me, and so it's just nice to have them there."

The young people we spoke with were very explicit about wanting to be treated with respect throughout the divorcing process. "I think sometimes parents just forget the kids are even there," said one teenager. "My mom is divorced, and she's dating a divorced man with a 12-year-old son. She was complaining to me about finding someone to stay with him so she and her boyfriend could go to the islands for New Year's. She said to me, 'Corey's a real problem. We always have to find a sitter for him when we travel.' I said, 'Mom, Corey's not a problem. Kids are never a problem. He's a *factor* or a *reason.*' She said, 'I didn't mean he's a problem. I meant that he gets in the way.' I said, 'Mom, kids don't get in the way.' I think that kids deserve to be a number one priority, and that sometimes parents lose that thought right after a divorce."

Several of those we interviewed disclosed that they felt great pleasure from looking at pictures or hearing happy stories from their parents about the parents' lives together before the divorce. Some said that there'd been so much bitterness between their parents for so many years that it had come as a wonderful emotional shock to them to find out that their parents had once been in love. "My father called me a week after Thanksgiving to tell me he was thinking about getting married again," reported a 20-year-old. "I said, 'Dad, you don't really sound sure about it.' He said, 'I don't think after the divorce I'll ever be sure again.' He went on to tell me how head over heels in love he'd been with my mother." The young person's eyes welled up with tears. "I couldn't believe it. Here he was, talking about how desperately in love he was with my mother. I thought, can this be? Is this real? But I knew that it was, and for the first time in my life I knew that he had loved her; that there was a time when she was a very important person to him. It meant so much to me." Many such poignant stories from these young people suggested there is an emotional need among children of divorce to assure themselves that at least at some point in their parents' lives those parents had fond feelings for one another.

We asked those we interviewed if they had any recommendations for divorcing parents that, if followed, might make the process of divorce less painful for other children going through it. Here are some of the suggestions they gave us:

- "Try not to talk about each other in a negative way in front of your kids. Keep your problems between yourselves."

- "Even though you're going to be apart, make an effort to get along. I mean, like anybody else; if you needed to get along with somebody at work or whatever. You know, just for the child, so the child can have both parents around. Just make an effort to get along."

- "It isn't fair when your mom says that if you love her you won't love your dad, or you have to love her more than you love your dad."

- "Try to get along better, or at least don't fight around the kids. If you're going to fight, do it when the kids aren't there. It would have been much easier for me if my parents had done that. Much, much easier. I couldn't believe they had so many things to yell at each other about. I mean, where do they get them?"

- "I think the main thing is to try and not involve your children in the middle when you're wanting to deal with your ex-spouse. Try and do it on your own. Don't try to get your children to do it for you, just because you don't want to have to deal with him. And just try and be as friendly as you can around each other so the children don't have to feel the stress of it. Talk to each other."

- "Allow the children to like the other parent. Make it OK to like the other parent. And if you don't like them, so what? Grin and bear it."

If one strong theme consistently emerged from our conversations with these young people, it was a desire to be allowed to love both parents equally without having to take sides. These children of divorce are not necessarily suggesting that divorced parents get along with each other, but merely that parents keep their disputes separate from their children's lives. In fact, *For the Sake of the Children* is not a book about abandoning conflict for the sake of peace, but instead is offered as a tool for conflict management and situational peace.

If you're divorcing, it is prudent to help your children redefine their concepts of "getting along," not as meaning "giving up" or "giving in," but as "giving it time"; to learn to negotiate a peaceful situation; to compromise not for the sake of compromise but to find a set of alternatives through which all parties can consider themselves winners. Divorce, by definition, is "not getting along," and our messages to young people to get along become a lesson in "do as I do, not as I say," unless we are clear that by "to get along" we mean that situations must be confronted, that anger must be managed and directed, and that mutually beneficial solutions must be invented or discovered and implemented.

Our children are not asking us to practice hypocrisy or to commit gross and unnatural acts for the sake of getting along. They are not asking us for conciliation when debate is needed, or for complacency to avoid making someone angry. They're not asking us to perpetuate intolerable situations or to allow ourselves to be emotionally blackmailed by others to avoid confrontation. They are simply asking us to manage our anger and conflict for the well-being of everyone, and to pick the proper time, place, and people.

It is up to us as the adults to see conflicting situations as an opportunity for growth, expansion, and development. There is no better opportunity to teach these skills to your children than when you find yourself in the situation of divorce.

Angelica was a 21-year-old college student when her parents divorced. Her father simply disappeared out of the family's life for almost a year. While he was going through a form of midlife crisis, her mother was going through her own torments from feelings of rejection and desertion.

It is now ten years later. Her parents never speak to each other unless they're thrown together at one of their children's big events such as a graduation or wedding, and then she says it is very uncomfortable for everyone.

Angelica was recently divorced herself. Here are some suggestions she shared with us for divorcing parents:

"Don't pit your kids against the other parent. I feel like I was cheated out of a father all through my twenties. Mom tried to transfer her bitterness toward him to us. I'd tell divorcing parents not to confuse the bitterness issues. Separate the marriage problems in your life from your life with your children.

"Tell your kids you love them, no matter what. I didn't think my dad loved me.

"For years I dealt with my mom's bitterness toward my dad. He's not perfect but . . . *he's my dad.* His betrayal was not of me. It was of her, if it did occur.

"You can't get over it. Now it's kind of backfired. I've reconciled with my dad. He did what he had to do. He maybe could have been more honest about it, but he's not a jerk. I feel like Mom cheated me. Now I feel anger at her, and I have to deal with that.

"My own divorce has brought back my parents' divorce very vividly. I feel abandoned and rejected, and I feel like, is this my *destiny?*"

▼

Chapter

10

How to Know When You Need Counseling

So far we have concentrated on the children of divorce and how parents can either destroy or support their children's attempts to deal with their new family structures. Consequently, we have focused on the relationship between the two divorced or divorcing people as parents, rather than as two people with a dissolved connection quite separate from their roles as fathers and mothers. This dissolution has its own consequences for the adults, of course. The dissolution of any relationship may cause depression, confusion, anger, or any number of other emotional reactions that need to be dealt with for the mental well-being of the people involved.

As we discussed throughout this book, it is vital for divorced couples to recognize the dissolution of the marriage and to work toward emotional detachment from one another. Part of this procedure involves grieving, a natural and necessary step in accepting any significant separation. Divorce presents a unique set of circumstances in that, while marriages dissolve, children do not. Therefore, the loss of a spouse through divorce produces a situation in which you are tied to this person, through your children, until one of you dies. *This is why it is important to recognize that you might go through a grieving process:* it will help you learn what to do about the positive feelings, as well as the negative feelings, that you have toward this person to whom you are no longer attached by marriage. Grief can facilitate the recovery stage of rebuilding your life.

The most direct action you can take to facilitate grieving is to consciously think about specific memories of your life with your former spouse over and over again. For instance, let's say you have particular memories of arguments you two had during which your former spouse said especially hurtful things to you. Replaying them repeatedly in your mind, in a constructive fashion geared toward learning from them, can make them less and less hurtful, until one day you will be able to think about them with very little emotion. (If you find after a year, however, that replaying painful memories only augments the pain, then it's time to get some help. Here the instruction and guidance of a counselor can help you put your situation into perspective, as discussed in detail later.) The same is true of fond memories, and it may be even more important to acknowledge these good memories. By doing this, you can gradually become desensitized, which can result in decreased emotional dependencies on your former spouse.

For example, suppose you and your former spouse had a favorite song that brings back special moments in your lives together. It might represent the first time you met, or a shared love of dancing, or the birth of a child. Whatever special memories it holds for you, it can be helpful for you to spend a quiet evening alone listening to this music, letting your emotions pour out into your pillow. You may even want to create a desirable setting for yourself in which to expunge your grief by lowering the light level or ordering some fresh flowers. It is advisable, however, that you have a friend or perhaps a sibling, or someone else that you trust, alerted that you may need him or her sometime during the process, and ask that he or she please be available by phone in case you need someone to talk to. Also, avoid taking any depressants, such as alcohol, when you're directing your memories toward your former spouse. Even though this process of mourning can be painful, it can help you to lessen your sensitivities about your former marriage partner, and thus better prepare you to adjust.

Note that grieving is a process, not an overnight remedy. It doesn't happen in the same way or with the same intensity for everyone; and it takes time. The more acknowledging and sorting out you can do, the sooner you can become less sensitive to your emotional ties.

What happens when you cannot adjust to the new demands life has presented you? Should you seek counseling? Some degree of depression and/or anxiety is natural when changes such as separation, divorce, or other losses present themselves. Knowing whether you can meet the challenge or whether you need to seek help is often difficult. Not just with counseling, but with many professional services it's difficult to judge when to seek professional help. How many of us have waited too long, hoping some problem would work itself out, only to find that we should have consulted someone weeks ago? Have you ever thought, "This cold will go away any day now," only to discover that the upper respiratory infection you had been enduring for weeks should have received the attention of a physician much sooner? Sometimes by the time we are prepared to ask for help it's either too late or the problem has grown so that it's going to be even harder to solve.

Yet most of us have times when we feel depressed, angry, confused, or frightened. These feelings are not always a sign that professional counseling is needed. Some people can adjust to divorce on their own; others can profit from therapy. Before giving you some "tips" on how to do a self-evaluation of whether or not you need counseling, it might be helpful to give you an idea of what "counseling" is, or should be. Often people fail to seek out therapy because of some misconception about the nature of counseling.

People most often seek out counseling when they become aware that they are not satisfactorily solving or coping with some personal or family problem. The term *counseling* is usually defined as "giving advice or advising." Because problems are seldom solved with advice, it might be more useful to think of counseling in terms of guidance of self—it is your relationship with your many "selves" that has come into question. After a brief personal history, the counselor might discuss with you what you expect to achieve in counseling. The two of you can set some standards for what constitutes "getting better." Without these criteria, you could be better and not know it, or feel better and not be. You'll learn some elementary psychology from the counselor that should help you understand some of the dynamics of "getting better." You'll get an introduction to general semantics that should help you understand the way language affects our view of ourselves and others. When there's something you don't understand, it's your responsibility to ask and discuss the issue.

It's also important to have homework. Homework is generally a set of experiences you and the counselor identify that gives you a chance to practice new behavior between sessions. If you don't practice the lessons you are

210

learning, it's hard for you to perfect them. Relief can be expected if you apply what you learn to everyday living. Not all counselors use homework as a technique. However, we strongly recommend it.

As you progress in counseling, realize that change is not only threatening but it also takes time. People progress in a sort of "two steps forward and one step back" style. Therefore, the key to success in counseling is to *apply* what you learn in your sessions to your daily life. That can be a frightening concept, but once you accept that the counselor cannot "fix" you, and that you are going to have to "fix" yourself through a guide, you have made the first big step toward getting better.

When you get into therapy, the counselor will spend a little time going over the specifics of what you perceive to be your problem. However, it should soon be apparent that you could spend months rehashing your complaints and gain little—except perhaps a lot of bills. To make progress, you need to learn to use the counselor for more than a sounding board. A good counselor is an instructor, a coach, and a guide who can help you learn new ways of interacting with your world more effectively.

Keep in mind that *your major task is to learn,* and in some cases, to *unlearn.* Often, in order to free up your mind for new information, it is important to unlearn some untruths that are blocking new growth. Three attitudes that seem to cause the most difficulty are (1) idealism, (2) an either–or approach to life, and (3) pride. Idealism is the belief that things must be a certain way and that anything short of the ideal is unacceptable. Examples of this kind of faulty thinking are "I must have a perfect nineteen-inch waist" or "I must have a successful marriage." We get our ideals from people we respect and look up to, and in doing so we sometimes assume that the ideals cannot be wrong, or that what is right for them must be applicable to us.

We need to always question our ideals and update them regularly.

The second way to short-circuit happiness is to approach life in an either–or manner. For example, you tell yourself, "either I have a nineteen-inch waist or I'm no good." Another example of this approach to life was demonstrated by Trudy. Trudy's father was an attorney, and she, her sister, and her two brothers were raised to believe that the only really acceptable vocation for them was to practice the law. Trudy also believed that she must, like her mother, marry a lawyer. Graduating in the top 1 percent of her high school class, she took the prelaw course in college, where she met and married another prelaw student. After completing undergraduate school, Trudy postponed getting her own law degree in order to put her husband through law school. Once he got his degree, they decided to start a family, and although Trudy did end up earning a master's degree, she never became an attorney. When her lawyer husband decided to leave her for someone younger, her feelings of self-worth and self-esteem were crushed. She not only felt worthless because of her failure to become a lawyer (which her other three siblings had accomplished), but also because she was now no longer married to an attorney. She greatly underrated her highly successful career in education and her nurturing skills with her children. Trudy needed counseling in order to see that her accomplishments were real and important, and that her either–or orientation to life was faulty and damaging.

The third crippler, pride, is such a powerful and potentially destructive human condition that to ever imagine that we have somehow overcome it is absurd. The most fearful thing about pride is that the more you have, the more invisible it is to you. To understand the dynamics of pride, it might be helpful to review what Sigmund Freud called defense mechanisms.

Defense Mechanisms

Defense mechanisms are those mental gymnastics that keep us from achieving insight about ourselves. Freud suggested that the ego has a way of protecting itself from pain and anxiety through these defense mechanisms, and that they become functional when they reduce anxiety or fear by unconsciously distorting reality. It is helpful to discuss these briefly:

- *Repression* is the process by which we get rid of unacceptable thoughts and feelings. It serves to hide or disguise anxiety-producing thoughts and feelings from conscious thought. After a divorce, for example, some people repress their anger toward their former spouse, refusing to acknowledge its existence.

- *Regression* lets us cope with fearful or anxious situations by retreating to an earlier, more secure time in our lives. For example, scared children on their first day of school find comfort in thumb sucking. In the case of divorce, some people scream, pout, and show other "hurt child" behavior toward their former spouses, rather than making a conscious effort to stay centered and focused on a particular issue that needs solving by two adults.

- *Reaction formation* lets the mind transform anxiety-producing thoughts or feelings into their opposite reactions. Hate becomes love. Feelings of insecurity become machismo. In the divorce process, some people transform their feelings of love, which are no longer acceptable, into indifference or rage, rather than working toward a healthy reattachment to the world.

- *Projection* contends that we attribute to others those things we fear about ourselves. We are able to avoid

213

accepting those traits in ourselves that we find objectionable. For instance, "He is stupid," may be a projection of one's own true feeling about oneself: "I feel stupid." A divorced parent who feels inadequate in his or her single parent role may think that his or her ex is being a poor parent.

- *Rationalization* allows us to offer self-justifying explanations for our own actions, thoughts, or behavior. For example, "I didn't make the child support payments this month because . . ." or "It's all right to berate my former spouse to our children because . . ." No matter how badly we behave, we can always rationalize our actions. This is a commonplace and regularly destructive type of behavior. Any sentence that contains the words *because* or *but* should be examined carefully for their roots in rationalization.

- *Displacement* allows us to divert our unacceptable urges toward a safer or more acceptable target than the person who tripped our trigger. Thus children who get yelled at often yell at the dog, because they can't appropriately direct their anger at the yelling parent. A divorced person may have an unrealistic worry about the effect of divorce on the children, which may actually be displaced fear about his or her own future.

- *Sublimation* allows us to redirect our anxieties and fears into acceptable tasks, causes, and endeavors. In that sense, sublimation lets us socially adapt. Busying ourselves with productive tasks, art, music, and the like directs our energies away from our internal pain. Similarly, a divorced person may suddenly become obsessed with religious work or the like.

According to Freud, defense mechanisms would not work if we were to recognize them for what they are. Once a person can see that he or she is using defense mechanisms, that person is then freed up to deal directly with the situation, and perhaps experience behavior change. The change, however, comes only through the experience of anxiety and fear and by learning to cope, think, and act differently. By acting differently, we can experience more effective behavior patterns and thus be less likely to use old, less effective problem-solving methods.

But we started by talking about pride. This detour through the wilds of defense mechanisms shows how defense mechanisms parallel the dynamics of pride. Pride by its very nature hides from its possessor, and in doing so perpetuates its existence. To get to the issue of *How to Overcome the Pitfall of Pride*, we must first, by necessity, break through our barriers of defensiveness:

- "Me? Too proud? I truly don't know what you're talking about." (*repression*)
- The behaviors of sulking or temper tantrums as a substitute for open and honest discussion about an issue, because you need to be "right." (*regression*)
- Holier-than-thou feelings or attitudes about those other people who have too much pride. (*projection*)
- Exaggerated humility. (*reaction formation*)
- "I deserve to be prideful because I am the best." (*rationalization*)

Until the "proud" owner acknowledges the state of affairs, no further change can take place. The owner is stuck with it, blind to the need for behavior change. So how do we break the sticky pattern of pride?

Recognition is the first step. If any of the preceding defense mechanisms sound like familiar behavior on your part, you are a good part of the way there. Entertain the idea for a moment that perhaps some pride on your part is contributing to noncommunication between you and your former spouse, or perpetuating some old battle, or fostering a never-ending cold war of silence. Just suppose for a minute (let's pretend), that it just might be you . . . or partially you. If you can get this far, then we're getting somewhere.

Now, just supposing it might be you (or someone who looks and acts a lot like you)—what's the next step in moving toward a situational peace?

Try taking the position (often taken by the stronger of two parties in a dispute) of owning up to responsibility for at least part of the conflict. The stronger of the parties may have the strength and sense of self-worth not only to own up to part of the discord but to go further, and take blame for the whole thing: "I'm sorry. This whole thing is my fault," *whether it is or not.* "I shouldn't have . . ." or "I should have . . ." and "What can I do to make this thing right with both of us?" Getting past the notion that somebody has to be at fault lays the groundwork on which to negotiate a situational peace. If two strong people are involved, the response to "It's all my fault," can likely be "No. It's all my fault" or "It's my fault, too." Fault having been assigned or accepted clears the way to set the ground rules for how each party will behave under the conditions of situational peace.

Even in the presence of only one strong person who is willing to accept the shortcoming, peace can still be attained. For example, suppose the response to "It's all my fault" is "Damn right it is. It's you, you, you, and let me tell you . . ." Once the haranguing stops, you can still both embark on a trek of situational peace, setting forth the wants and desires of each person, outlining some strategies for achieving a win–win situation, and setting forth some time lines to put the process into motion.

216

However, for those who suffer from lack of self-worth and self-esteem, life's challenges can be very difficult. No matter how hard we try, there may come a time when we are unprepared to overcome the hardships of our situations, from lack of experience or lack of energy, or perhaps because we are so enmeshed in the problem that the solutions are not obvious.

Asking for help is difficult. Most of us have been taught that we should solve our own problems or that asking for help is "a sign of a weak person." So we keep plugging away, repeating the same old mistakes. Chances are, if you are asking yourself if you should see a counselor, you probably should. It's a good sign that you may be accepting the fact that you are not solving your own problems. In any case, a good counselor can help you evaluate your own need for professional help. Some people who set up initial consultations with counselors are perfectly capable of working out their problems on their own, and merely need the reassurance of hearing it from a professional. Others may need additional guidance.

The following self-evaluation quiz is designed to help you decide if you need therapy. Be as introspective as you can be.

"SHOULD I SEE A COUNSELOR?"

If you think you need to, you probably do. If you've been thinking, "Should I see a counselor?" give yourself five points. If you've never considered it, give yourself zero points.

"AM I TRYING TO DEAL WITH THE SAME OLD PROBLEMS?"

Are you constantly trying to solve the same old problems in the same old ways? How many times before

---

have you been caught in the merry-go-round of problem solving? If this is not the first time you've tried unsuccessfully to solve this same problem, give yourself three points. If it's the same problem, but you are trying a new solution that you are prepared to abandon if it doesn't work, give yourself two points. If you've never seen this problem before, give yourself zero points.

"DO I HAVE HIGH SELF-ESTEEM?"

Do you usually look at your weaknesses rather than at your strengths? Are you consistently comparing yourself to others, feeling either totally less or more valuable than they? Do you always put the wishes and desires of others before your own? Do you go from day to day thinking that you can handle anything and everything, and then suddenly switch to a feeling of dread that you can't handle anything at all? If you answered no to all these questions, then you probably have a high, healthy self-esteem. Give yourself zero points. If you answered yes to some of these questions, give yourself two points. If you answered yes to most or all of these questions, give yourself three points. If you don't know how many points to give yourself here, try three.

"HAS MY ACTIVITY LEVEL CHANGED DRASTICALLY?"

Do you tend to sit around feeling lifeless and anxious, or attack situations at a frantic but unproductive pace? Are you unable to concentrate on any given project? Is your behavior out of sync with your goals? Do you feel overcome by exhaustion? If these scenarios describe you, give yourself three points. If you feel you are somewhat productive, give yourself two points. If you feel you are very productive without exhaustion, give yourself zero points.

"ARE MY RELATIONSHIPS FALLING APART?"

Do you feel that friends, workmates, neighbors, and family are "pulling away" from you? Do you find yourself more vulnerable than usual? The best test for this is to ask people who are likely to be honest with you. If they tell you they've noticed a change, give yourself three points. If they cannot give you a definite answer, give yourself two points. If they assure you they've noticed no difference (for instance, if they say, "Why did you ask?"), give yourself zero points. If you have no friends or family that you feel close enough to to ask, give yourself three points. If you ask a so-called honest group, and they protest too much that you're OK and that nothing is wrong, disqualify their responses, and give yourself three points.

TOTAL SCORE

- If you scored between ten and seventeen points, it's worth your time and money to get a more objective assessment than a self-test. *Go see a counselor.*

- If you scored between five and nine points, hang on and take the self-test again in a few days or weeks to see if the score has changed. If you are still fighting the same old problems, the score will soon go up. If it stays the same, keep your options open.

- If you scored less than five points, you're probably capable of working out your own problems, but it's still a good idea to keep tabs on how you're doing.

Above all, don't view the possibility of needing to see a counselor as some sign of weakness or defect in you. *It's the strong that have the courage to ask for help.* If you find yourself *repeatedly* feeling that the situation is out of control and you simply can't take it anymore, consider counseling . . . and the *key* here is repetition. We don't mean just a single isolated instance of frustration, but frustration over an event or issue that repeats itself. Any sign that the situation is not being resolved, by time and growth or by all-around problem solving, indicates that a therapist might help bring some objectivity to the scene.

Greta is an example of someone who was out of control. She was forty years old and the mother of a young son and three college-age kids when her husband left her. Suddenly, she stopped eating. Within six months, Greta had lost her teaching position because she couldn't focus on her job. She described her condition: "Initially I couldn't function at all. Before [the divorce] I was really able to concentrate. I was really one to jump in with enthusiasm to do a job. After he left me, I would always be distracted. My mind would wander. I would forget things. I wasn't doing a top-notch job. I couldn't even remember to eat."

She said she felt no anger at her former husband, even though he left her very abruptly after moving the family into a much smaller house in a different neighborhood. "I only felt anger at the situation I was in. Not at him. I felt a loss of status. I was scared. I felt pain. The way I handled it at the time was to run. I was out every night. I couldn't stand the four walls here," she said, looking around her attractively furnished dining room. "I didn't know the neighbors, and I felt very much deserted. I was out all the time, and I left my son by himself most of the time. It was a terrible thing to do, but I couldn't stand it. I would go out just about seven nights a week. I felt compelled to just flit off and make sure that the world out there loved me because I'd been rejected at home."

Greta needed counseling (as by now did her son). She was unable to recognize the anger she felt toward her former husband. She was dysfunctional at work, and lost her job. Her parenting was suffering because she was running away from her feelings by running away from home. Her self-esteem was acutely low. Her activity level was unfocused and unproductive. Her attempts to raise her self-esteem put her on a merry-go-round of problem-solving failures. These are all signs that indicate that therapy would be useful.

Involvement with drugs is another sign that you need help. If you find that your major way of coping is to take more alcohol, sedatives, or any controlled substance, seek help immediately. Seeking comfort in chemicals is dangerous and unproductive.

Deviant behavior on your part—behavior that exceeds the bounds of your own values or of social norms—also indicates a probable need for counseling. Atypical promiscuity (male or female) is a good sign that counseling might be in order. If your behavior doesn't feel right to you, you might want to talk it over with an objective third party. When you can't solve your problems yourself, ask for help.

What do you do if you feel you can't afford it? Most of us find that we can afford the things we really want, like cars, TVs, sport-specific footwear, and facial makeup. It's really a matter of valuing something so much that we are willing to make the necessary arrangements to get it. Unfortunately, we often put so low a value on our own selves or our own emotional well-being that we put those values below acquisition of CD players on our priority list. If you find yourself saying that you cannot afford counseling, ask yourself the following questions:

1. Have I checked with those agencies that offer a sliding fee scale? Am I aware of what the cost really

is? (Short-term therapy is often less expensive than a new TV, and certainly less expensive than a new car.)

2. Do I really want to change, or am I afraid to change? (Often we cling stubbornly to a bad deal because fear of the unknown is more frightening than hanging onto a bad deal.)

Divorce can create very stressful circumstances. Anger and hostility are often a part of divorce. These feelings are not always bad, and can be healthy if directed and managed in a healthy way. Sometimes it's reassuring to talk with an objective professional, even if we don't feel we're losing control. At other times, counseling is crucial. We sometimes get so caught up in a situation that we have no insight. In such emotional storms, a professional can help us understand where we are caught up in the dynamics of a relationship or situation.

How to Tell When Your Children Need Counseling

The ideal in a divorce is that everyone—Mom, Dad, and the kids—get some group counseling; they all sit down together and identify their new roles in the changing family structure. This helps children clarify how they fit into the divorcing process and helps them understand the situation.

As the children of divorce discussed in the previous chapter, often the kids just don't grasp the situation, even when the parents sit down and explain it to them. They may deny it, misunderstand it, or simply blow it off. Involving a good counselor in the discussion makes it *real* to the children. A good counselor can help sort out who isn't getting the message, and can clarify it, while Mom,

Dad, and the children are all so close to it that they have their own biases.

If one parent simply refuses to attend counseling, then the other parent should accompany the children. One parent is better than none. The least beneficial (although better than nothing) is for parents to simply dump the children off at the counselor's (like your parents may have dumped you off at Sunday school). It's best when all attend together.

Children are entitled to a certain amount of anger, sadness, and fear as players in a divorcing family. For the first six months to a year, children do their own grieving. As the end of the first year approaches, children who are resolving their grief have fewer outpourings of tears, anger, sadness, or tantrums. After the first year, behavior to watch for from your children that may indicate a need for therapy include failure to express anger or sorrow where these feelings are appropriate, and displays of far more resentment or sadness than situations seem to call for. Another sign to watch for is a behavior change from your child, such as when a child stops functioning: refusing to do tasks around the house, failing to complete homework assignments, or having problems with his or her friends at school.

As children enter adolescence and hormonal and social upheavals begin to affect their lives, insecurity, anger, fear, uncertainty, and a host of other emotions may flow freely, often without purpose or destination.

In divorcing families, the normal, though aggravating tensions of adolescence are confused and sometimes made worse by the tensions and uncertainties of the divorce and by the changes in living, social, and often financial conditions. For teenagers of divorce, two powerful emotional environments are at work. Although you as a parent should not necessarily overread hostility and conflict on the part of the child as rejection because of the divorce, when perhaps it's based in hormones and adolescence, never-theless it may be a good idea to seek counseling for your teenager when you feel the situation is out of control. Once it becomes apparent that the problem is not being resolved, it's time to seek the help of a good counselor.

Other signs to watch for in your teenagers are

1. Withdrawal from school activities and peers.

2. Attempts to gain social acceptance or to cope with tension by involvement with alcohol or other drugs.

3. Deviant behavior that exceeds the bounds of social norms. (If your kids are staying out until 3 A.M. and that doesn't feel right to you, find out what the standard is for the school or neighborhood.)

Once you decide that counseling is called for, don't make it a litigation issue in the divorce. If each parent takes the child to his or her own therapist, it can lead to confusion and mixed messages for the child. Look for a good, competent counselor, using the techniques discussed in Chapter 8, and then follow through with that therapist.

Also, don't make therapy for your child a money issue. If the courts have not decided who will pay for what, and the child is not covered by insurance, then a good rule of thumb to follow is that each parent pays according to the percentage of his or her combined net income (after bills, expenses, and so on). If one parent makes 80 per-cent of the net income, then that parent pays 80 percent of the cost of the child's counseling.

One particularly ugly example of how *not* to handle a child's needs involved 17-year-old Jeff. Jeff's father, a powerful attorney in the Midwest, sought custody of his son when the child was 5 years old. Jeff didn't want to live with his dad, and being forced from his mother's home left him feeling helpless—as though he had no control over his own life. Once his father got custody of Jeff, he lost interest in the child, leaving him pretty much to his own devices. By the time Jeff was 7 or 8, he'd become a little bully in school, learning to manipulate his teachers and peers. He longed for control of his own life.

When Jeff turned 14, he moved back in with his mother. He saw this as the answer to all his wishes, and believed that from here on out he could control his own life. By this time, Jeff was encumbered with the baggage of rage he carried from his past experiences. He refused to accept any attempts by his mother to put restrictions on his behavior, and turned to alcohol as a way of coping with his anger and frustration.

Finally, just as Jeff turned 17, he was involved in an incident that forced his mother's hand. He was faced with a choice of going to jail, or entering a private rehabilitation program. He chose the program.

When Jeff had moved out of his father's home two years before, his dad had let the medical insurance he carried on his son lapse. Now faced with medical bills of $23,000 a month, plus doctor's fees and medication charges, Jeff's mother turned to the only source she knew for a loan: her former parents-in-law. They, in turn, forced Jeff's father to do the right thing and take financial responsibility for the medical bills.

After three months in a hospital in Arizona, Jeff was transferred to a residential facility in Oklahoma. As Jeff's father was checking him into the facility, he told his son, "You know, this money will come out of *your* inheritance."

Jeff now feels that something else is being taken away from him. He feels guilt for the anger he holds toward his father, and his feelings of hatred are eating him alive. He experiences terrible grief, justifies his violent behavior, abuses alcohol, and doesn't see himself as behaving any differently from anyone else. He suffers from acutely low self-esteem. Jeff's chances for recovery become less and less with each experience of failure. Although Jeff's case is more severe than most, it demonstrates the conflict that can arise when parents refuse to cooperate in the best interest of the child.

In summary, if you think you or your children might profit from therapy, consult a counselor about it. Think of it as preventive medicine. One consultation won't hurt you, and it may help.

Happy Endings, New Beginnings

Happy Endings

Alexandra is a woman of striking self-confidence and high self-esteem. At 49, she is attractive, well educated, and reasonably satisfied with her life. According to her, this was not always the case.

At the time of her divorce, which took place ten years ago, her four children were 16, 15, 13, and 7. She says of those times, "There was a separation before we actually proceeded with the divorce, and I was totally unprepared for the amount of anger and bitterness that came after the separation. I suppose it was a naive assumption on my part that he would go his way and I would go my way, and we'd somehow negotiate for the welfare of the children. I had no idea the rage that both of us felt about the expectations we'd had about each other. We would eventually have to deal with those expectations."

Alexandra describes herself as having been on the wrong track with the wrong man. She says their whole relationship had been based on control . . . his control of her. "Total control," she says, "not anything else. And when somebody lets go of the control, you have this feeling that you're out of control.

"For the first time in my life I'd begun to develop my own identity, and when I started to realize who I was, it was too much of a change for George. One day I was fixing dinner and he was arguing one more time and I remember to this day gritting my teeth really hard and saying, 'If you don't like it, then you should leave.' And he did."

Alexandra says of the children that there had been a lot of stress in the family, so that when George left the house there was some relief for them from the strain. "Instead of bringing out the best, or enhancing one another, George and I brought out the worst in each other. Because it was a control thing, it ended up being a battered wife situation where there were threats of physical punishment, coercion, that kind of thing. I found out later the kids were aware of it, although I didn't think so at the time."

The issue of money still seems to provoke Alexandra. "Child support was supposed to be $50 per week per child. I had no support at all. I couldn't count on George for anything, to the point I can't talk about it yet. After a while I just gave up. Too much hassle. You can't make someone be a responsible person. He did sign over a vested interest in some property we owned together, but that was it."

As to what the children think about their mother taking full financial responsibility for them, Alexandra says, "I think it's beyond rational thinking. *The kids love their dad,* apart from anything else. Respect is another whole issue. They *love* their dad. They don't want to have to defend him, so we don't get into discussions about it. They've seen me rage. They've seen him rage. They've been through

228

it all. They just *love* their dad, no matter what he does or doesn't do."

Alexandra says she still feels anger when she thinks about the time their youngest son moved in with his father. "He took over Teddy's custody. I used to get calls from Ted at one o'clock in the morning. He'd have a fever, and he would have no idea where his dad was. Ted stayed with his dad for nine months before he moved back in with my present husband and me. I was overjoyed, but it wasn't best that he had to make that decision."

She says there was a lot of manipulation from the children to get her and George to act as a family unit. "Now we do holidays together. We have for several years. I think the kids get a kick out of George and my becoming parents again. It's stopped what I call the divorce syndrome. You know, the kids don't run between us anymore. They're free to do what they want to and have relationships independently with each of us. It's made a difference."

Their son, Ted, says that he's happy about the way it is now, but that he can remember when it was really bad. "I do remember when it was tense and tight, but now it feels like that was such a brief period in my life," he says. "I'm used to everyone spending time together, and I like it that way. It feels like this is the way it's always been. I like being able to have all my family together at once. Now it's like, everything's so great, hey, why doesn't everybody go out and get a divorce and have one, big extended family," he declares laughingly.

Alexandra says she thinks there's a certain equation that has to happen before divorced parents can once again share holidays with the children together. "I think a certain amount of time has to pass, so that you can have a chance to have made it in your own world. There's a kind of confidence that you have to have within yourself . . . somewhere in there . . . before you can go in and take on the old tough stuff again. You know, you have to have your own self-esteem built in, because if you look at that person and say, 'That's what you did,' or 'That's what you didn't do,' then you're still playing the old game. You're playing the old tapes. It's got to be beyond that. And you had good times, too, that you can concentrate on. I mean, they weren't all bad times. I was married eighteen years to this person. There are good memories if you look for them. You have to have that kind of attitude, you know? You have to have your own space and feel good about it."

She says they usually spend between two and four days together over the holidays, often on neutral ground. "It creates a third space. For example, last year at Christmas we rented a house in Vermont. The family package was a ski trip. Everyone, children, grandchildren, George, his woman friend, my husband and I, all came up and stayed and kind of bunked in. Everybody contributed a little bit—a dollar, some food—a little bit of everything. George was a big help. We'd created this third area that's not mine nor his. It makes it very easy, to work in those kinds of spaces. My issues are often not George, but going back to the full-time 'Mom' after not being that for a while. You know, taking care of the grandkids. My issues are sometimes more the kids than him."

Alexandra says they don't necessarily avoid discussing things that might lend themselves to disagreements, but that initially she did. "It used to be that George would tell his version of something, or express his views, and for the sake of the family I would never say anything. That has changed. Now I'll say, 'Look, George, if you really want to discuss this, I would like to be able to say that that's not the way I understand the problem. Now we can talk about it here in front of everyone, we can postpone the discussion until a later time, or we can just drop it.' I don't let it pass the way I used to in order to have him back in the family after all this. I wouldn't have said something like that three years ago. This Christmas I said it quite frequently. At the same time, it's not with anger or animosity . . . even five years ago, I'd have said, 'Why you . . . you're lying, man,' which is what I'd have been thinking. It's a constantly evolving situation. It just goes on."

George and Alexandra did both attend the children's big events together before they started sharing holidays, but she says it was different. "I mean, you have this little juggling act; what your feelings are versus what you do for somebody else. I don't know that we ever verbalized rules, but they kind of showed up. What you do talk about and what you don't. Stay in the present. In the moment. You can get through a few of those times."

She described the first couple of holidays that they spent together as a blended family. "I can remember, George was very supportive. He'd help fix vegetables, for example, and the first couple of times I thought, 'Where in the *hell* did this come from,' you know? You go through that, wondering why he wasn't like this before. But the other side of it is, spending this time in such close proximity with him, it reassured me that I'd made the right move terminating our marriage."

It was Alexandra who approached George about getting the whole family back together. "I just said to him, 'You know, we couldn't make a marriage, but boy, don't we have swell kids? I'd like to think that we did something wonderful together. I don't want the kids to feel like, when they have children, that they have to have a grandparents' weekend every other weekend. One for you and one for me. I'd like them to know that if I walk in, and you're there, fine. If you walk in and I'm there, great. You know, we've got this thing of grandparenting to share. I'm going to love those grandchildren. You're going to love those grandchildren. And they're from us. You know, you can't separate that. There's part of you in that child, and there's part of me. I'm not going to reject any part of that baby. Let's enjoy the good stuff. Get off the bad stuff.' George felt pretty much the same way."

Alexandra acknowledges that she had a role model to go by. "When George's younger brother got married in 1968, his father came back from California, married again, to go to his son's wedding. George's parents hadn't seen each other in twenty years, and everyone was full of trepidation about what was going to happen when Jacob saw Anne again. They were at our house, and they walked outside, into my backyard, and started to shake hands, and then hugged. Inadvertently hugged. And the role model was created. After that I always invited both of George's parents and their present spouses for Christmas, and they came, and it was wonderful, so I kind of had a role model to go by."

Hopefully Alexandra and George will become role models for other divorced parents and help them recognize the importance children place on their divorced parents' attitudes toward each other.

New Beginnings

Candy's first child was born when she was 41. She and Dennis had been trying to have a child from the first day of their six-year marriage. Candy went through two surgeries, gave up one ovary and one tube, and went on fertility pills in order to conceive. The important issue here is to note the intensity of emotion, time, energy, and money that Candy and Dennis put into having a baby. It is not an understatement to say that the first six years of the marriage had its entire basis in procreation. Clearly, a child was an important aspect of their marriage. Ironically, in retrospect, Candy says her pregnancy was the beginning of the end of their marriage.

Because of the delicacy of the pregnancy, intercourse was not advised during the first several months of pregnancy. Candy reflected, "I thought that once I got past the point where I probably wouldn't miscarry, that our sexual relations would pick up again. I just wasn't worried about it, and so sex ended, and we never had it again. Ever. I excused it because I was pregnant."

Because Dennis had his own business, Candy says she didn't think much about it when he began staying at the office longer and longer into the evenings. "He was always coming home late, and I had to be at work early, so he began sleeping on the couch when he'd get home so he wouldn't wake me. It was probably stupid on my part, but I just didn't think that much about it."

She says that she continued to find excuses for his absences. "Allen was born, and Dennis didn't even spend much time at the hospital. He even worked on Thanksgiving Day. Allen and I were still in the hospital, and my friends came by. I just didn't realize what was happening. Then when I came home, I was just kind of euphoric. It was the Christmas season, and here I was with the baby, and, you know, people were coming by. It was just like I always dreamed it would be, except that Dennis wasn't in the picture. He just wasn't there."

After six weeks, Candy went back to work. She'd given birth by cesarean section, which was her third major surgery in a four-year span. "I was really tired, and would have liked Dennis's help. Finally I confronted him. I said, 'I feel like we're just never together anymore,' and he dropped the bomb. 'You know,' he said, 'My feelings have changed.'"

Candy paused for a long time before continuing, "You know, he was telling me he didn't want to be married. The worst part came after that, because I started to fall apart. I couldn't eat. I couldn't sleep. I felt like everything I had hoped for and dreamed of was unraveling, and that, in my mind, it was like the whole family thing was blown apart, and I wasn't going to get to keep Allen."

At this point, Candy's eyes welled as she continued. "I think because I got so low there were a couple of times when it crossed my mind that I didn't know whether I wanted to live. As I understand it from my counselor, that thought crosses everybody's mind sometime or other, but it scared me. I mean, it's not like I wanted to do anything about it, but I was so distraught I just wanted to get rid of the pain. I think what I really wanted was some rest, because I remember saying, 'I need to go into a hospital or something for a couple of days and just be knocked out.' The more discombobulated I got, the further Dennis distanced himself."

She recognized she needed some help, and Dennis said he wanted to participate. "We started going to counseling at my suggestion, and Dennis played a game with me. He lied. He lied to the counselor, and he lied to me. Maybe he was lying to himself. In the meantime I kept functioning at work and everything; no one at work knew what was going on. But *for me*, I was a wreck. Anyway, Dennis lied and said he wanted to stay together. He said he wanted to work it out, but he really didn't. That came out later. We never resumed our sex life, and he continued to sleep on the couch. It got to the point where he was just kind of living there, sponging off of me. I mean, that's the way I saw it, because he wasn't putting anything into the situation at all. Not even financially. I owned the house when we got married. So finally, after two months of heavy grieving, and I mean *heavy duty*, you know, the rage finally started setting in. And the grief stopped. I don't know what kicked it in, but finally I just got so angry and so enraged at him for pursuing the pregnancy and then just abandoning the whole situation, I told him, 'You're just taking advantage of me. You don't want me in this picture,' and so he left."

Just when Candy thought things were getting easier for her to handle, Dennis decided to fight her on the issue of custody. He was basing his claims on the two-month period following Allen's birth when he'd said he wanted out of the marriage and she'd become distraught. "He was going to use it against me in court. He did put it into a deposition. He was going to tell a judge that he feared if there was another crisis in my life that I wouldn't be a fit parent. Instability. And then I guess maybe I proved myself to him, or maybe he just ran out of money. Perhaps his lawyer told him it was a ridiculous claim because, if you look at my mental health record or my work record, you'd know he'd have never gotten anywhere with it. Anyway, he gave it up. I think what he'd been afraid of was that if I got sole custody that he'd be denied the things that he wanted, but as time went on he realized that he wasn't going to be denied visitation or anything."

Candy says that the marriage almost cost her her house because of a trust deed she'd signed during their marriage for a business loan for Dennis's company. When the loan became due and he didn't have the money, the bank wanted to foreclose. Although she ended up keeping her house, it cost her $10,000 to do it.

However, in spite of the emotional and financial traumas that Candy has been through in her relationship with Dennis, she says, "I've put forth a monumental effort to remove my feelings about everything that he's done and all the rage and everything, and I just keep trying to focus all the time on dealing with him *only* as Allen's father. The counselor we were seeing told us, as soon as Dennis acknowledged that he wanted out of the marriage, that what we did to each other and how we treated each other and dealt with one another for the first six months during our separation would be vital, because it would set a precedent for how everything would work out for us as parents. That stuck in my mind, and I thought, 'Yeah, that's true.' Consequently, I put aside all the other stuff as best I could, and I've tried not to get into fights with Dennis or argue with him because I figured it would set a pattern. If we got really down and dirty, then it would be much harder to deal with him. So I don't. I just try and stay as emotionally removed from him as I can. I never ask him anything about himself or his personal life or how he's doing. I never show any interest in him personally. I just try and stay very calm and businesslike. I treat it as a business arrangement where there's a task to be done."

Candy said they do discuss Allen enough to get by, but she's aware that as he gets older they'll probably need to discuss him more. "We discuss his health and some of his developments. I tell him when we go to the zoo and things like that, primarily so he knows what I'm doing with him. I know we'll have to discuss him more in the future, but I just can't do it yet."

She says she intends never to talk Dennis down to Allen. "I'm really aware of the damage that that can do. I want the two of them to have a relationship. I want it to be a good relationship. I want Allen to feel loved by as many people as he can. Also, I'm hoping against hope that Dennis is going to be a better father than he was a husband, and he may be. I mean, I view him as totally irresponsible, but when he's with Allen he's certainly loving and all that. As far as dealing with Dennis, I think the best way for me to deal with him is to keep it very emotionless. Don't get mad. Don't get hurt. Don't do any of that stuff, because it won't work if you do, and it only creates a bigger problem than whatever it is we're discussing. We were in disagreement over visitation during Labor Day weekend. When it got to the point where we were butting heads, I said, 'Let's just stop. This is getting to be where we're just both being stubborn. Now we each want our own way. Let's just make our decision based on what's best for him. That's what this whole thing's about, not whether

236

you're getting your way or I'm getting my way.' And he said, 'Yeah, you're right.'"

Candy says that, for her, the key to communicating and cooperating with her child's father is to keep factual, emotionless, and businesslike. She says she thinks this strategy is the least exhausting and the most productive, not just for the parents, but for kids, too, because they see their parents working together in a kind of harmony rather than discord. "That's got to be good for children for a lot of reasons. It avoids putting them through the misery of watching two people argue all the time, and they also have an opportunity to see two people cooperating and working together in this kind of a situation."

Candy's philosophy on divorced parenting will go a long way in helping to create for her son a healthy, happy environment in which he will be more able to love both parents without guilt. By learning to break her emotional attachment to Dennis, Candy frees herself to participate in whatever cooperation is necessary to coparent their son. By showing forgiving behavior, she sets an example for Allen that may help him through some of the tough times he'll face in his own life.

Children need and deserve to be allowed to love both parents without having to take sides. They shouldn't have to feel that they're always in the middle between their parents, trying to negotiate for the right to love them both. They should be free of the financial responsibilities and disputes involved in their upbringing. They should be able to attend the important events in their lives without fear of parental discord. They shouldn't have to be manipulative or dishonest in order to enjoy their heritage.

Once you can recognize the dissolution of the marriage between you and your former spouse, you can work toward achieving emotional detachment from that person and taking more active control of your thoughts and behavior. The techniques and strategies in this book offer you the tools to learn how to focus on your job as a mother or father and how to deal with your children's perceptions of their other parent. In spite of your anger, you can learn how to share your children with your ex-spouse, and doing so will help them flourish in their modified family structure.

Index